Foundations of Freemasonry Series

THE PHILOSOPHY OF MASONRY IN FIVE PARTS

Foundations of Freemasonry Series

THE PHILOSOPHY OF MASONRY
Five Lectures
Delivered under the Auspices of the Grand Master of Massachusetts, Masonic Temple, Boston

By Roscoe Pound,
Professor of Jurisprudence in Harvard University

Lamp of Trismegistus
NEW YORK . GENEVA . BEIJING
WELLINGTON . KANSAS CITY

Copyright © 2013 Lamp of Trismegistus

All rights reserved. No part of this publication may be reproduced or transmitted in any form or by any means, electronic or mechanical, including photocopying, recording, or by any information storage and retrieval system, without permission in writing from Lamp of Trismegistus. Reviewers may quote brief passages.

ISBN: 978-1-63118-004-0

PART I
WILLIAM PRESTON

Philosophers are by no means agreed with respect to the scope and subject matter of philosophy. Nor are Masonic scholars at one with respect to the scope and purpose of Freemasonry. Hence one may not expect to define and delimit Masonic philosophy according to the easy method of Dickens' editor who wrote upon Chinese metaphysics by reading in the Encyclopedia upon China and upon metaphysics and combining his information. It is enough to say at the outset that in the sense in which philosophers of Masonry have used the term, philosophy is the science of fundamentals. Possibly it would be more correct to think of the philosophy of Masonry as organized Masonic knowledge--as a system of Masonic knowledge. But there has come to be a well-defined branch of Masonic learning which has to do with certain fundamental questions; and these fundamental questions may be called the problems of Masonic philosophy, since that branch of Masonic learning which treats of them has been called commonly the philosophy of Masonry. These fundamental questions are three:

1) What is the nature and purpose of Masonry as an institution? For what does it exist? What does it seek to do? Of course for the philosopher this involves also and chiefly the questions, what ought Masonry to be? For what ought it to exist? What ought it to seek as its end?

2) What is- and this involves what should be- the relation of Masonry to other human institutions, especially to those directed toward similar ends? What is its place in a rational scheme of human activities?

3) What are the fundamental principles by which Masonry is governed in attaining the end it seeks? This again, to the philosopher, involves the question what those principles ought to be.

Four eminent Masonic scholars have essayed to answer these questions and in so doing have given us four systems of Masonic philosophy, namely, William Preston, Karl Christian Friedrich Krause, George Oliver and Albert Pike. Of these four systems of Masonic philosophy, two, if I may put it so, are intellectual systems. They appeal to and are based upon reason only. These two are the system of Preston and that of Krause. The other two are, if I may put it that way, spiritual systems. They do not flow from the rationalism of the eighteenth century but spring instead from a reaction toward the mystic ideas of the hermetic philosophers in the seventeenth century. As I shall try to show here-after, this is characteristic of each, though much more marked in one.

Summarily, then, we have four systems of Masonic philosophy. Two are intellectual systems: First that of Preston, whose key word is Knowledge; second, that of Krause, whose key word is Morals. Two are spiritual systems: First that of Oliver, whose key word is Tradition; and second, that of Pike, whose key word is Symbolism.

Comparing the two intellectual systems of Masonic philosophy, the intrinsic importance of Preston's is much less than that of Krause's. Krause's philosophy of Masonry has a very high value in and of itself. On the other hand the chief interest in Preston's philosophy of Masonry, apart from his historical position among Masonic philosophers, is to be found in the circumstance that his philosophy is the philosophy of our American lectures and hence is the only one with which the average American Mason acquires any familiarity.

Preston was not, like Krause, a man in advance of his time who taught his own time and the future. He was thoroughly a child of his time. Hence to understand his writings we must know the man and the time. Accordingly I shall divide this discourse into three parts:
1) The man
2) the time
3) Preston's philosophy of Masonry as a product of the two.

First, then, the man. William Preston was born at Edinburgh on August 7,1742. His father was a writer to the signet or solicitor-- the lower branch of the legal profession--and seems to have been a man of some education and ability. At any rate he sent William to the high school at Edinburgh, the caliber of which in those days may be judged from the circumstance that the boy entered it at six- -though he was thought very precocious. At school he made some progress in Latin and even began Greek. But all this was at an early age. His father died while William was a mere boy and he was taken out of school, apparently before he was twelve years old. His father had left him to the care of Thomas Ruddiman, a well-known linguist and he became the latter's clerk. Later Ruddiman apprenticed William to his brother who was a printer, so that Preston learned the printer's trade as a boy of fourteen or fifteen. On the death of his patron (apparently having nothing by inheritance from his father) Preston went into the printing shop as an apprentice and worked there as a journeyman until 1762. In that year, with the consent of the master to whom he had been apprenticed, he went to London. He was only eighteen years old, but carried a letter to the king's printer, and so found employment at once. He remained in the employ of the latter during substantially the whole remaining period of his life.

Preston's abilities showed themselves in the printing shop from the beginning. He not merely set up the matter at which he worked but he contrived in some way to read it and to think about it. From setting up the great variety of matter which came to the king's printer he acquired a notable literary style and became known to the authors whose books and writings he helped to set up as a judge of style and as a critic. Accordingly he was made proof reader and corrector for the press and worked as such during the greater part of his career. He did work of this sort on the writings of Gibbon, Hume, Robertson and authors of that rank, and presentation copies of the works of these authors, which were found among Preston's effects at his death, attest the value which they put upon the labors of the printer.

Preston had no more than come of age when he was made a Mason in a lodge of Scotchmen in London. This lodge had attempted to get a warrant from the Grand Lodge of Scotland, but that body very properly refused to invade London, and the Scotch petitioners turned to the Grand Lodge of Ancients, by whom they were chartered. Thus Preston was made in the system of his great rival, Dermott, just as the latter was at first affiliated with a regular or modern lodge. According to the English usage, which permits simultaneous membership in several lodges, Preston presently became a member of a lodge subordinate to the older Grand Lodge. Something here converted him, and he persuaded the lodge in which he had been raised to secede from the Ancients and to be reconstituted by the so-called Moderns. Thus he cast his lot definitely with the latter and soon became their most redoubtable champion. Be it remembered that the Preston who did all this was a young man of twenty-three and a journeyman printer.

At the age of twenty-five he became master of the newly constituted lodge, and as such conceived it his duty to make a thorough study of the Masonic institution. His own words are worth quoting:

"When I first had the honor to be elected master of a lodge, I thought it proper to inform myself fully of the general rules of the society, that I might be able to fulfill my own duty and officially enforce obedience in others. The methods which I adopted with this view excited in some of superficial knowledge an absolute dislike of what they considered as innovations, and in others, who were better informed, a jealousy of preeminence which the principles of Masonry ought have checked. Notwithstanding these discouragements, however, I persevered in my intention."

Indeed one cannot wonder that the pretenses of this journeyman printer of twenty-five were scouted by older Masons. But for the present Preston had to contend with nothing more than shakings of the head. Unlike the scholarly, philosophical, imperturbable, academic Krause, Preston was a fighter. Probably his confident dogmatism, which shows itself throughout his lectures, his aggressiveness and his ambition made more enemies than the supposed innovations involved in his Masonic research. Moreover we must not forget that he had to overcome three very serious obstacles namely, dependence for his daily bread upon a trade at which he worked twelve hours a day, youth, and recent connection with the fraternity. That Preston was not persecuted at this stage of his career and that he succeeded in taking the lead as he did is a complete testimony to his abilities.

Preston had three great qualifications for the work he undertook:

1) Indefatigable diligence, whereby he found

time and means to read everything that bore on Masonry after twelve hours of work at his trade daily, six days in the week

2) a marvelous memory, which no detail of his reading ever escaped

3) a great power of making friends and of enlisting their enthusiastic co-operation.

He utilized this last resource abundantly, corresponding diligently all with well-informed Masons abroad and taking advantage of every opportunity to interview Masons at home. The results of this communication with all the prominent Masons of his time are to be seen in his lectures.

It was a bold but most timely step when this youthful master of a new lodge determined to rewrite or rather to write the lectures of Craft Masonry. The old charges had been read to the initiate originally, and from this there had grown up a practice of orally expounding their contents and commenting upon the important points. To turn this into a system of fixed lectures and give them a definite place in the ritual was a much-needed step in the development of the work. But it was so distinctly a step that the ease with which it was achieved is quite as striking as the result itself.

When Preston began the composition of his lectures, he organized a sort of club, composed of his friends, for the purpose of listening to him and criticizing him. This club was wont to meet twice a week in order to pass on, criticize and learn the lecture as Preston conceived it. Finally in 1772, after seven years, he interested the grand lodge officers in his work and delivered an oration, which appears in the first edition of his Illustrations of Masonry, before a meeting of eminent Masons including the principal grand officers. After delivery of the oration, he expounded his system to the meeting. His hearers approved the lectures, and, though official sanction was not given immediately, the result was to give them a standing which insured their ultimate success. His disciples began now to go about from lodge to lodge delivering his lectures and to come back to the weekly meetings with criticisms and suggestions. Thus by 1774 his system was complete. He then instituted a regular school of instruction, which obtained the sanction of the Grand Lodge and thus diffused his lectures throughout England. This made him the most prominent Mason of the time, so that he was elected to the famous Lodge of Antiquity, one of the four old lodges of 1717, and the one which claimed Sir Christopher Wren for a past master. He was soon elected master of this lodge and continued such for many years, giving the lodge a pre-eminent place in English Masonry which it has kept ever since.

Preston's Masonic career, however, was not one of unbroken triumph. In 1779 his views as to Masonic history and Masonic jurisprudence brought him into conflict with the Grand Lodge. It is hard to get at the exact facts in the mass of controversial writing which this dispute brought forth. Fairly stated, they seem to have been about as follows:

The Grand Lodge had a rule against lodges going in public processions. The Lodge of Antiquity determined on St. John's Day, 1777, to go in a body to St. Dunstan's church, a few steps only from the lodge room. Some of the members protested against this as being in conflict with the rule of the Grand Lodge, and in consequence only ten attended. These ten clothed themselves in the vestry of the church, sat in the same pew during the service and sermon, and then walked across the street to the lodge room in their gloves and aprons. This action gave rise to a debate in the lodge at its next meeting, and in the debate Preston expressed the opinion that the Lodge of Antiquity, which was older than the Grand Lodge and had participated in its formation, had certain inherent privileges, and that it had never lost its right to go in procession as it had done in 1694 before there was any Grand Lodge. Thus far the controversy may remind us of the recent differences between Bro. Pitts and the Grand Lodge authorities in Michigan. But the authority of Grand Lodges was too recent at that time to make it expedient to overlook such doctrine when announced by the first Masonic scholar of the day. Hence, for maintaining this opinion, Preston was expelled by the Grand Lodge, and in consequence the Lodge of Antiquity severed its connection with the Grand Lodge of Moderns and entered into relations with the revived Grand Lodge at York. The breach was not healed till 1787.

Upon settlement of the controversy with the Grand Lodge of Moderns, Preston, restored to all his honors and dignities, at once resumed his Masonic activities. Among other things, he organized a society of Masonic scholars, the first of its kind. It was known as the Order of the Harodim and included the most distinguished Masons of the time. Preston taught his lectures in this society, and through it they came to America, where they are the foundation of our Craft lectures. Unhappily at the Union in England in 1813 his lectures were displaced by those of Hemming, which critics concur in pronouncing much inferior. But Preston was ill at the time and seems to have taken no part whatever in the negotiations that led to the Union nor in the Union itself. He died in 1818, at the age of 76, after a lingering illness. A diligent and frugal life had enabled him to lay by some money and he was able to leave 800 pounds for Masonic uses, 500 pounds to the Freemason's charity for orphans--for which, left an orphan himself before the age of twelve, he had a natural sympathy-- and 300 pounds to endow the so-called Prestonian lecture--an annual lecture in Preston's words verbatim by a lecturer appointed by the Grand Lodge. This lecture is still kept up and serves to remind us that Preston was the first to insist on the minute verbal accuracy which is now a feature of our lectures. It should be noted also that in addition to his lectures, Preston's book, Illustrations of Masonry, has had great influence. It went through some twenty editions in England, four or five in America, and two in Germany.

So much for the man.

Now as to the time.

Three striking characteristics of the first three quarters of the eighteenth century in England are of importance for an understanding of Preston's philosophy of Masonry:

1) It was a period of mental quiescence

2) both in England and elsewhere it was a period of formal over-refinement

3) it was the so-called age of reason, when the intellect was taken to be self-sufficient and men were sure that knowledge was a panacea.

In contrast with the seventeenth century, the eighteenth century was a period of quiescence. Society had ceased to be in a state of furious ebullition, nor was there a conflict of manifestly irreconcilable ideas as in the time just gone by. On the surface there was harmony. True, as the events of the end of the century showed, it was a harmony of compromise rather than of reconciliation--a truce, not a peace. But men ceased for a time to quarrel over fundamentals and turned their attention to details and to form. A common theological philosophy was accepted by men who denounced each other heartily for comparatively trivial differences of opinion. In politics, Whig and Tory had become little more than names, and both parties agreed to accept, with little modification, the body of doctrine afterwards known as the principles of the English Revolution. Political ideas were fixed. Men conceived of a social compact from which every detail of social and political rights and duties might be deduced by abstract reasoning and believed that it was possible in this way to work out a model code for the legislator, a touchstone of sound law for the judge and an infallible guide to private conduct for the individual. In literature and in art there was a like acquiescence in accepted canons. A certain supposed classical style was assumed to be the final and the only permissible mode of expression. In other words acquiescence was the dominant tendency and finality was the dominant idea. For example, Blackstone, a true representative of the century, thought complacently of the legal system of his time, with its heavy load of archaisms, almost ripe for the legislative reform movement of the next generation, as substantially perfect. Nothing, so he thought, was left for the completion of five hundred years of legal development but to patch up a few trivial details. In the same spirit of finality the framers of our bills of rights undertook to lay out legal and political charts for all time. Indeed the absolute legal philosophy of our text books which has made so much trouble for the social reformers of yesterday and of today, speaks from the eighteenth century. In this spirit of finality, with this same confidence that his time had the key to reason and could pronounce once for all for every time, for every place and for every people, Preston framed the dogmatic discourses which we are content to take as the lectures of Freemasonry.

    For the modern world, the eighteenth century was par excellence the period of formalism. It was the period of formal over-refinement in every department of human activity. It was the age of formal verse and heroic diction, of a classical school in art which lost sight of the spirit in reproducing the forms of antiquity, of elaborate and involved court etiquette, of formal diplomacy, of the Red Tape and Circumlocution Office in every portion of administration, of formal military tactics in which efficiency in the field yielded to the exigencies of parade and soldiers went into the field dressed for the ball room. Our insistence upon letter perfect, phonographic reproduction of the ritual comes from this period, and Preston fastened that idea upon our lectures, perhaps for all time.

The third circumstance, that the eighteenth century was the era of purely intellectualist philosophy naturally determined Preston's philosophy of Masonry. At that time reason was the central idea of all philosophical thought. Knowledge was regarded as the universal solvent. Hence when Preston found in his old lectures that among other things Masonry was a body of knowledge and discovered in the old charges a history of knowledge and of its transmission from antiquity, it was inevitable that he make knowledge the central point of his system. How thoroughly he did this is apparent today in our American Fellowcraft lecture, which, with all the abridgments to which it has been subjected, is still essentially Prestonian. Time does not suffice to read Preston in his original rhetorical prolixity. But a few examples from Webb's version, which at these points is only an abridgment, will serve to make the point. The quotations are from a Webb monitor, but have been compared in each case with an authentic version of Preston.

"The Globes are two artificial spherical bodies, on the convex surface of which are represented the countries, seas, and various parts of the earth, the face of the heavens, the planetary revolutions, and other particulars.

"The sphere, with the parts of the earth delineated on its surface, is called the Terrestrial Globe; and that with the constellations, and other heavenly bodies, the Celestial Globe.

"The principal use of the Globes, besides serving as maps to distinguish the outward parts of the earth, and the situation of the fixed stars, is to illustrate and explain the phenomena arising from the annual revolution and the diurnal rotation of the earth around its own axis. They are the noblest instruments for improving the mind, and giving it the most distinct idea of any problem or proposition, as well as enabling it to solve the same."

It has often been pointed out that these globe on the pillars are pure anachronisms. They are due to Preston's desire to make the Masonic lectures teach astronomy, which just then was the dominant science.

Note particularly the purpose, as the lecture sets it forth expressly: "for improving the mind and for giving it the most distinct idea of any problem or proposition as well as enabling it to solve the same."

In other words, these globes are not symbolic,

they are not designed for moral improvement. They rest upon the pillars, grotesquely out of place, simply and solely to teach the lodge the elements of geography and astronomy.

We must remember that Preston, who worked twelve hours a day setting type or reading proof, would look on this very differently from the Mason of today. What are commonplaces of science now were by no means general property then. To him the teaching of the globes was a perfectly serious matter.

Turn to the solemn disquisition on architecture in our Fellowcraft lecture. As we give it, it is unadulterated Preston, but happily it is often much abridged. You know how it runs, how it describes each order in detail, gives the proportions, tells what was the model, appends an artistic critique, and sets forth the legend of the invention of the Corinthian order by Callimachus. The foundation for all this is in the old charges. But in Preston's hands it has become simply a treatise on architecture. The Mason who listened to it repeatedly would become a learned man. He would know what an educated man ought to know about the orders of architecture.

In the same way he gives us an abridgment of Euclid:

"Geometry treats of the powers and properties of magnitudes in general, where length, breadth and thickness are considered, from a point to a line, from a line to a superficies, and from a superficies to a solid. A point is a dimensionless figure, or an indivisible part of space. A line is a point continued, and a figure of one capacity, namely, length. A superficies is a figure of two dimensions, namely, length and breadth. A solid is a figure of three dimensions, namely, length, breadth and thickness."

But enough of this. You see the design. By making the lectures epitomes of all the great branches of learning, the Masonic Lodge may be made a school in which all men, before the days of public schools and wide-open universities, might acquire knowledge, by which alone they could achieve all things. If all men had knowledge, so Preston thought, all human, all social problems would be solved. With knowledge on which to proceed deductively, human reason would obviate the need of government and of force and an era of perfection would be at hand. But those were the days of endowed schools which were not for the many. The priceless solvent, knowledge, was out of reach of the common run of men who most needed it. Hence to Preston, first and above all else the Masonic order existed to propagate and diffuse knowledge. To this end, therefore, he seized upon the opportunity afforded by the lectures and sought by means of them to develop in an intelligent whole all the knowledge of his day.

Now that knowledge has become too vast to be comprised in any one scheme and too protean to be formulated as to any of its details even for the brief life of a modern text, the defects of such a scheme are obvious enough. That this was Preston's conception, may be shown abundantly from his lectures. For instance:

"Smelling is that sense by which we distinguish odors, the various kinds of which convey different opinions to the mind. Animal and vegetable bodies, and, indeed, most other bodies, while exposed to the air, continually send forth effluvia of vast subtlety, as well in the state of life and growth, as in the state of fermentation and putrefaction. These effluvia, being drawn into the nostrils along with the air, are the means by which all bodies are smelled."

This bit of eighteenth-century physics, which makes us smile today, is still gravely recited in many of our lodges as if it had some real or some symbolic importance. It means simply that Preston was endeavoring to write a primer of physiology and of physics.

He states his theory expressly in these words:

"On the mind all our knowledge must depend; what, therefore, can be a more proper subject for the investigation of Masons ? By anatomical dissection and observation we become acquainted with the body; but it is by the anatomy of the mind alone we discover its powers and principles."

That is: All knowledge depends upon the mind. Hence the Mason should study the mind as the instrument of acquiring knowledge, the one thing needful.

Today this seems a narrow and inadequate conception. But the basis of such a philosophy of Masonry is perfectly clear if we remember the man and the time. We must think of these lectures as the work of a printer, the son of an educated father, but taken from school before he was twelve and condemned to pick up what he could from the manuscripts he set up in the shop or by tireless labor at night after a full day's work. We must think of them as the work of a laborer, chiefly self-educated, associated with the great literati of the time whom he came to know through preparing their manuscripts for the press and reading their proofs, and so filled with their enthusiasm for enlightenment in what men thought the age of reason. We must think of them as the work of one imbued with the cardinal notions of the time--intellectualism, the all-sufficiency of reason, the absolute need of knowledge as the basis on which reason proceeds, and finality.

How, then, does Preston answer the three problems of Masonic philosophy?

1) For what does Masonry exist? What is the end and purpose of the order? Preston would answer: To diffuse light, that is, to spread knowledge among men. This, he might say, is the proximate end. He might agree with Krause that the ultimate purpose is to perfect men--to make them better, wiser and consequently happier. But the means of achieving this perfection, he would say, is general diffusion of knowledge. Hence, he would say, above all things Masonry exists to promote knowledge; the Mason ought first of all to cultivate his mind, he ought to study the liberal arts and sciences; he ought to become a learned man.

2) What is the relation of Masonry to other human activities? Preston does not answer this

question directly anywhere in his writings. But we may gather that he would have said something like this: The state seeks to make men better and happier by preserving order. The church seeks this end by cultivating the moral person and by holding in the background supernatural sanctions. Masonry endeavors to make men better and happier by teaching them and by diffusing knowledge among them. This, bear in mind, was before education of the masses had become a function of the state.

3) How does Masonry seek to achieve its purposes? What are the principles by which it is governed in attaining its end?

Preston answers that both by symbols and by lectures the Mason is (first) admonished to study and to acquire learning and (second) actually taught a complete system of organized knowledge. We have his own words for both of these ideas. As to the first, in his system both lectures and charges reiterate it. For example: "The study of the liberal arts, that valuable branch of education which tends so effectually to polish and adorn the mind is earnestly recommended to your consideration." Again, notice how he dwells upon the advantages of each art as he expounds it:

"Grammar teaches the proper arrangement of words according to the idiom or dialect of any particular people, and that excellency of pronunciation which enables us to speak or write a language with accuracy, agreeably to reason and correct usage. Rhetoric teaches us to speak copiously and fluently on any subject, not merely with propriety alone, but with all the advantages of force and elegance, wisely contriving to captivate the hearer by strength of argument and beauty of expression, whether it be to entreat and exhort, to admonish or applaud."

As to the second proposition, one example will suffice:

"Tools and implements of architecture are selected by the fraternity to imprint on the memory wise and serious truths."

In other words the purpose even of the symbols is to teach wise and serious truths. The word serious here is significant. It is palpably a hit at those of his brethren who were inclined to be mystics and to dabble in what Preston regarded as the empty jargon of the hermetic philosophers.

Finally, to show his estimate of what he was doing and hence what, in his view, Masonic lectures should be, he says himself of his Fellowcraft lecture: "This lecture contains a regular system of science [note that science then meant knowledge] demonstrated on the clearest principles and established on the firmest foundation."

One need not say that we cannot accept the Prestonian philosophy of Masonry as sufficient for the Masons of today. Much less can we accept the details or even the general framework of his ambitious scheme to expound all knowledge and set forth a complete outline of a liberal education in three lectures. We need not wonder that Masonic philosophy has made so little headway in Anglo-

American Masonry when we reflect that this is what we have been brought up on and that it is all that most Masons ever hear of. It comes with an official sanction that seems to preclude inquiry, and we forget the purpose of it in its obsolete details. But I suspect we do Preston a great injustice in thus preserving the literal terms of the lectures at the expense of their fundamental idea. In his day they did teach-- today they do not. Suppose today a man of Preston's tireless diligence attempted a new set of lectures which should unify knowledge and present its essentials so that the ordinary man could comprehend them. To use Preston's words, suppose lectures were written, as a result of seven years of labor, and the co-operation of a society of critics, which set forth a regular system of modern knowledge demonstrated on the clearest principles and established on the firmest foundation. Suppose, if you will, that this were confined simply to knowledge of Masonry. Would not Preston's real idea (in an age of public schools) be more truly carried than by our present lip service, and would not his central notion of the lodge as a center of light vindicate itself by its results?

    Let me give two examples. In Preston's day, there was a general need, from which Preston had suffered, of popular education--of providing the means whereby the common man could acquire knowledge in general. Today there is no less general need of a special kind of knowledge. Society is divided sharply into classes that understand each other none too well and hence are getting wholly out of sympathy. What nobler Masonic lecture could there be than one which took up the fundamenta of social science and undertook to spread a sound knowledge of it among all Masons ? Suppose such a lecture was composed, as Preston's lectures were, was tried on by delivery in lodge after lodge, as his were, and after criticism and recasting as a result of years of labor, was taught to all our masters. Would not our lodges diffuse a real light in the community and take a great step forward in their work of making for human perfection?

Again, in spite of what is happening for the moment upon the Continent, this is an era of universality and internationality. The thinking world is tending strongly to insist upon breaking over narrow local boundaries and upon looking at things from a world-wide point of view. Art, science, economics, labor and fraternal organizations, and even sport are tending to become international. The growing frequency of international congresses and conferences upon all manner of subjects emphasizes this breaking of local political bonds. The sociological movement, the world over, is causing men to take a broader and more humane view, is causing them to think more of society and hence more of the world-society, is causing them to focus their vision less upon the individual, and hence less upon the individual locality.

In this world-wide movement toward universality Masons ought to take the lead. But how much does the busy Mason know, much less think, of the movement for internationality or even the pacifist movement which has been going forward all about him? Yet every Mason ought to know these things and ought to take them to heart. Every lodge ought to be a center of light from which men go forth filled with new ideas of social justice, cosmopolitan justice and internationality.

Preston of course was wrong--knowledge is not the sole end of Masonry. But in another way Preston was right. Knowledge is one end--at least one proximate end--and it is not the least of those by which human perfection shall be attained. Preston's mistakes were the mistakes of his century--the mistake of faith in the finality of what was known to that era, and the mistake of regarding correct formal presentation as the one sound method of instruction. But what shall be said of the greater mistake we make today, when we go on reciting his lectures--shorn and abridged till they mean nothing to the hearer--and gravely presenting them as a system of Masonic knowledge ? Bear in mind, he thought of them as presenting a general scheme of knowledge, not as a system of purely Masonic information. If we were governed by his spirit, understood the root idea of his philosophy and had but half his zeal and diligence, surely we could make our lectures and through them our lodges a real force in society. Here indeed, we should encounter the precisians and formalists of whom lodges have always been full, and should be charged with innovation. But Preston was called an innovator. And he was one in the sense that he put new lectures in the place of the old reading of the Gothic constitutions. Preston encountered the same precisians and the same formalists and wrote our lectures in their despite. I hate to think that all initiative is gone from our order and that no new Preston will arise to take up his conception of Knowledge as an end of the fraternity and present to the Masons of today the knowledge which they ought to possess.

PART II
KRAUSE

Except as he builds upon the old charges and so uses older materials, Preston speaks so completely from the eighteenth century that one needs but understand the thinking of eighteenth-century England to appreciate him fully. In the case of our next Masonic philosopher, there is another story. He was in the main current of the philosophical thought of his day. But that current, along with the current of Masonic thought, had been flowing without break from the seventeenth century. Hence to appraise his philosophy of Masonry it is not enough to consider the man and the time. We must begin farther back.

The beginning of the seventeenth century was a period of great mental activity. The awakening of the Reformation had brought in an era of fresh and vigorous religious thought. Political ideas foreshadowing those of the eighteenth and nineteenth centuries were taking form. The downfall of scholasticism had set philosophy free from Aristotle. Grotius was about to emancipate Jurisprudence from Theology. Corning was about to deliver Law from Justinian. In consequence a new theory of law and government arose. Men went back to the classical Roman jurists and their law of nature founded on reason--applicable to men, not as citizens, nor as members of civilized society, but simply and solely as men--and the philosophical school which resulted and maintained itself during the two succeeding centuries, produced the great succession of publicists, who built up the system of international law, launched the ever-growing movement for humanity in war and ultimate peace, and stimulated that interest in legal and political philosophy, of which the democratic ideas of our own time, and the humanizing and rationalizing of law in the nineteenth century, were to be the fruit. The renascence of Masonry, complete in the next century, had its roots in this period. "There was always," says Sir Henry Maine, "a close association between Natural Law and humanity." In such a time, with the very air full of ideas of human brotherhood and of the rational claims of humanity, the notion of an organization of all men, for the general welfare of mankind, was to be looked for. It may be seen, indeed, in the opening years of the century; and we need not doubt that the writings of Andreae and the well-known Rosicrucian controversy were a symptom rather than a cause. But the idea was slow in attaining its maturity. In the seventeenth century, it struggled beneath a load of alchemy and mysticism, bequeathed to it by an obsolete era of ignorance and superstition. In the eighteenth century, it was retarded by the absorbing interest in political philosophy. Hence it was not till the first decade of the nineteenth century that the possibilities of this phase of the new thought were perceived entirely. Then, for the first time, the idea of general organization of mankind was treated in scientific method, referred to a definite end, and made part of a philosophical system of human activities. Perhaps no better theme could be chosen as an introduction to Masonic philosophy, than the life and work of that learned and eminent man and Mason, in his time at once the first of Masonic philosophers and the foremost of philosophers of law, who rendered this service to humanity and to the Craft.

Karl Christian Friedrich Krause, one of the founders of a new Masonic literature, and the founder of a school of legal thought, was born at Eisenberg, not far from Leipzig, in 1781. He was educated at Jena, where he taught for some time, till, in 1805, he removed to Dresden. In this same year, he became a Mason; and at once, with characteristic energy and enthusiasm, he entered upon a critical and philosophical study of the institution, reading every Masonic work accessible. As a result of his studies, he delivered twelve lectures before his lodge in Diesden, which were published in 1809, under the title: "Hoehere Vergeistung der echtuberlieferten Grundsymbole der Freirmaurerei," or "Higher Spiritualization of the True Symbols of Masonry." A year later, he published the first volume of his great work, "Die drei aeltesten Kunsturkunden del Freimaurerbruderschaft," or "The Three Oldest Professional Records of the Masonic Fraternity." This book, in the words of Dr. Mackey, "one of the most learned that ever issued from the Masonic press," unhappily fell upon evil days. The limits of permissible public discussion of Masonic symbols were then uncertain, and the liberty of the individual Mason to interpret them for himself, since expounded so eloquently by Albert Pike, was not wholly conceded by the German Masons of that day. In consequence he met the fate which has befallen so many of the great scholars of the Craft. His name, even more than those of Preston and Dalcho and Crucefix and Oliver, warns us that honest ignorance, zealous bigotry, and well-meaning intolerance are to be found even among sincere and fraternal seekers for the light. The very rumor of Krause's book produced great agitation. Extraordinary efforts were made to prevent its publication, and, when these failed, the mistaken zeal of his contemporaries was exerted toward expelling him from the order. Not only was he excommunicated by his lodge, but the persecution to which his Masonic publications gave rise clung to him all his life, and prevented him from receiving public recognition of the position he occupied among the thinkers of his day. It has been said, indeed, that he was too far in advance of the time to be understood fully beyond a small circle of friends and disciples. Yet there seems no doubt that the bitterness engendered by the Masonic controversies over his book was chiefly instrumental in preventing him from attaining a professorship. Happily, he was not a man to yield to persecution or misfortune. Like the poet, he might have said," *** I seek not good-fortune, I myself am good fortune."

Undaunted by miscomprehension of his teachings, unembittered by the seeming success of his energies, he labored steadily, as a lecturer at the

University of Goettingen, in the development and dissemination of the system of legal and political philosophy from which his fame is derived. Roeder has recorded the deep impression which his lectures left upon the hearers, and the common opinion which placed him far above the respectable mediocrities who held professorships in the institution, where he was a simple docent. As we read the accounts of his work as a lecturer, and turn over the earnest, devout, and tolerant pages of his books, full of faith in the perfectibility of man, and of zeal discovering and furthering the conditions of human progress, we must needs feel that here was one prepared in his heart and made by nature, from whom no judgment of a lodge could permanently divide us. He died in 1832 at the relatively early age of 51.

Krause did not leave us a complete or systematic exposition of his general philosophical system. Nor can it be said that he achieved much of moment in the field of philosophy at large, though some historians of philosophy accord him a notable place. It is rather in the special fields of the philosophy of Masonry, to which he devoted the enthusiasm of youth, and of the philosophy of law, to which he turned his maturer energies, that he will be remembered. In the latter field, indeed, he is still a force. Two able and zealous disciples, Ahrens and Roeder, labored for more than a generation in expounding and spreading his doctrines. The great work of Ahrens, published five years after his master's death, has gone through twenty-four editions, in seven languages. Thus Krause became recognized as the founder of a school of legal and political philosophers, and his followers, not merely by writings, but by meetings and congresses, developed and disseminated his ideas. Until the rise of the military spirit in Germany and the shifting of the growing point of German law to legislation, produced a new order of ideas, the influence of his doctrines was almost dominant. Outside of Germany, especially in lands where the philosophy of law is yet a virgin field, they still have a useful and fruitful future before them, and he has been pronounced the "leader of the latest and largest thought" in the sphere of legal philosophy. In view of the social-philosophical and sociological movements in the last generation, this characterization is no longer accurate. But it is true that until the rise of the great names of the social- philosophical school of legal thought in the past decade, Krause's was the greatest name in modern legal philosophy. His great Masonic work is disfigured by the uncritical voracity, characteristic of Masonic writers until a very recent period, which led him to give an unhesitating credence to tradition, and to accept, as genuine, documents of doubtful authenticity, or even downright fabrications. Hence his historical and philological investigations, in which he minutely examines the so-called Leland MS., the Entered Apprentice Lecture, and the so-called York Constitutions, as well as his dissertation on the form of government and administration in the Masonic order, must be read with caution, and with many allowances for over-credulity. But in spite of these blemishes--and they unhappily disfigure too large a portion of the historical and critical literature of the Craft--his Masonic writings are invaluable.

In a time and among a people in which the nineteenth-century indifference to philosophy is exceptionally strong, and threatens to deprive Law and Government, Jurisprudence and Politics of all basis, other than popular caprice, a teaching which sets them on a surer and more enduring ground, which seeks to direct them to a definite place and to give them definite work in a general scheme of human progress, cannot fail to be tonic. For the Mason, however, Krause's system of legal philosophy has a further and higher value. It is not merely that his works on the philosophy of law, written, for the most part, after his period of Masonic research and Masonic authorship was at an end, afford us, at many points, memorable examples of the practical possibilities of Masonic studies. Nor is it merely that he enforces so strenuously the social, political, and legal applications of the principles of our lectures. His great achievement, his chiefest title to our enduring gratitude, is the organic theory of law and the state, in which he develops the seventeenth-century notion of a general organization of mankind into a practical doctrine, seeks to unite the state with all other groups and organizations--high or low, whatever their immediate scope or purpose--in a harmonious system of men's activities, and points out the station and the objective of our world-wide brotherhood in the line of battle of human progress. Let me indicate to you some of the leading points of his Masonic and of his legal philosophy, and the relation of the one to the other.

Law is but "the skeleton of social order, clothed upon by the flesh and blood of morality." Among primitive peoples, it is no more than a device to keep the peace, and to regulate, so far as may be, the archaic remedy of private war. In time it is taken over by the state, and is able to put down violence, where originally it could go no farther than to limit it. This done, it may aspire to a better end, and seek not only to preserve order but to do justice. Thus far it has come at present. But beyond all this, says Krause, there is a higher and nobler goal, which is, he says, "The perfection of man and of society." The law, singly, is by no means adequate to this task. Rightly understood, it is one of many agencies, which are to operate harmoniously, each in its own sphere, toward that great end. The state organizes and wields but one of these agencies. Morals, religion, science, the arts, industry and commerce--all these, in his view, are co-workers, and must be organized also. But the state, or the political organization, being charged with the duty of maintaining the development of justice, has the special function of assuring to the other forms of organized human activity the means of perfecting themselves. It must "mediate between the individual and the social destiny." Thus it is but an organ in the whole social organism. He looks upon human society as an organic whole, made up of many diverse institutions, each related to an important phase of human life, and all destined, at an epoch of maturity, to compose a superior unity. Relatively, they are independent. In a wider view and looked at with an eye to the ultimate result, they are parts of a single mechanism. All operate in one direction and to one end-- the achievement of the destiny of humanity, which is perfection. Nor is this idle speculation. Krause seeks to animate these several phases of human activity, these varied institutions evolved as organs of the social body, with a new spirit. He impresses upon us that we are not on the decline, but are rather in a period of youth. Humanity, he insists, is but beginning to acquire the consciousness of its social aim. Knowing its aim, conscious of the high perfection that awaits it, he calls upon mankind, by harmonious development of its institutions, to reach the ideal through conscious development of the real.

This insistence upon perfection as a social aim and upon conscious striving to that end is of capital importance in contrast with the ideas which prevailed so generally in the latter half of the nineteenth century. Under the influence of the positivists and of the mechanical sociologists for a time there was a condition of social, political and juristic pessimism. Men thought of society as governed by the inflexible operation of fixed social laws, whose workings we might observe, as we may observe the workings of the law of gravitation in the motions of the heavenly bodies, but might no more influence in the one case than in the other. Krause's social philosophy, on the other hand, to use a recent phrase, gives us faith in the efficacy of effort and thus accords with the best tendencies of social and political thought in the present.

Krause's philosophy of Masonry and his philosophy of law require us to distinguish the natural order, the social order and the moral order. The distinction may be developed as follows.

Scientists tell us that nature exhibits a ceaseless and relentless strife--a struggle for existence, though this way of putting it had not been invented in Krause's day--in which all individuals, races, and species are inevitably involved. The very weeds by the roadside are not only at war with one another for room to grow, but must contend for their existence against the ravages of insects, the voracity of grazing animals, and the implements of men. Thus, the staple of life, under purely natural conditions, is conflict. If we turn to the artificial conditions of a garden, the contrast is extreme. Exotics, which-could not maintain themselves a moment, in an alien soil and an unwonted climate, against the competition of hardy native weeds, thrive luxuriantly. Planted carefully, so as not to interfere with each other, carefully tended, so as to eliminate the competition of native vegetation, supplied with the best of soil, watered whenever the natural supply is deficient, the individual plants, freed from the natural necessity of caring for themselves in the struggle for existence, turn their whole energies to more perfect development, and produce forms and varieties of which their rude, uncultivated originals scarcely convey a hint. All struggle for existence is not eliminated, indeed, in the garden. But the burden of it is shifted. Instead of each plant struggling with every other for a precarious existence the gardener contends with nature for the existence of his garden. He covers his plants to protect from frosts, he waters them to mitigate drought, he sprays them to prevent injury by insects, and he hoes to keep down the competition of weeds. Instead of leaving each plant to propagate itself as it may, he gathers and selects the seed, prepares the ground, and sows so as to insure the best results. The whole proceeding is at variance with nature; and it is maintained only by continual strife with nature, and at the price of vigilance and diligence. If these are relaxed, insects, drought, and weeds soon gain the day, and the artificial order of the garden is at an end.

Society and civilization are, in like manner, an artificial order, maintained at the price of vigilance and diligence in opposition to natural forces. As in the garden, so in society, the characteristic feature is elimination of the struggle for existence, by removal or amelioration of the conditions which give rise to it. On the other hand, in savage or primitive society, as in the natural plant society of the wayside, the characteristic feature is the intense and unending competition of the struggle for existence. In the wayside weed patch, nature exerts herself to adjust the forms of life to the conditions of existence. In the garden, the gardener strives to adjust the conditions of existence to the forms of life he intends to cultivate. Similarly, among savage and uncivilized races, men adjust themselves as they may to a harsh environment. With the advent and development of society and civilization, men-create an artificial environment, adjusted to their needs and furthering their continued progress. Thus, the social and moral ordeal are, in a sense, artificial; they have been set up in opposition to the natural order, and they are maintained and maintainable only by strife with nature, and the repression of natural instincts and primitive desires. It has been said that nature is morally indifferent. Morality is a conception which belongs to the social, not to the natural existence. The course of conduct which the member of civilized society pursues would be fatal to the savage; and the course followed by the savage would be fatal to society. The savage, like any wild animal, fights out the struggle for existence relentlessly. The civilized man joins his best energies to those of his fellows, in the endeavor to limit and eliminate that struggle.

The social ordeal, then, is, as it were, an artificial order, set up and maintained by the cooperation of numbers of individuals through successive generations. Just as the garden demands vigilance and diligence on the part of the gardener, to prevent the encroachment and re-establishment of the natural order, so the social order requires continual struggle with natural surroundings, as well as with other societies and with individuals, wherewith its interests or necessities come in conflict. Consequently, in addition to the instincts of self and species preservation, there is required an instinct or intuition of preserving and maintaining the social order. Whether we regard this as acquired in an orderly process of evolution, or as implanted in man at creation, it stands as the basis of right and justice, bringing about as a moral habit, "that tendency of the will and mode of conduct which refrains from disturbing the lives and interests of others, and, as far as possible, hinders such interference on the part of others." The mere knowledge by individuals, however, that the welfare, and even the continuance, of society require each to limit his activities somewhat with reference to the activities of others, does not suffice to keep within the bounds required by-right and justice. The more primitive and powerful selfish instincts tend to prevail in action. Hence private war was an ordinary process of archaic society. The competing activities of individuals could not be brought into harmony and were left to adjust themselves. But peace, order, and security are essential to civilization. Every individual must be relieved from the necessity of guarding his interests against encroachment, and set free to pursue some special end with his whole energies. As civilization advances, this is done by substituting the force of society for that of the individual, and thus putting an end to private war. Historically, law grew up to this demand.

The maintenance of society and the promotion

of its welfare, however, as has been seen, depend upon much besides the law. Even in its original and more humble role of preserving the peace, the law was by no means the first in importance. The germs of legal institutions are to be seen in ancient religions, and religion and morals held men in check while law was yet in embryo. Beginning as one, religion, morals and law have slowly differentiated into the three regulating and controlling agencies by which right and justice are upheld and society is made possible. In many respects their aim is common, in many respects they cover the same field, among some peoples they are still confused, in whole or in part. But today, among enlightened peoples, they stand as three great systems; with their own aims, their own fields, their own organization, and their own methods; each keeping down the atavistic tendencies toward wrong-doing and private war, and each bearing its share in the support of the artificial social order, by maintaining right and justice. Religion governs men, so far as it is a regulating agency, supernatural sanctions; morality by the sanction of private conscience, fortified by public opinion; law by the sanction of the force of organized society. Each, therefore, to be able to employ its sanctions systematically and effectively in maintaining society, must be directed or wielded by an organization. Accordingly we find the church giving regulative and coercive force to religion and the state taking over and putting itself behind the law. But what is behind the third of these great agencies? What and where is the organization that gives system and effectiveness to the regulative force of morality?

Here, Krause tells us, is the post of the Masonic order. World-wide; respecting every honest creed, requiring adherence to none; teaching obedience to states, but confining itself to no one of them; it looks to religion on the one side and to law upon the other, and, standing upon the solid middle-ground of the universal moral sentiments of mankind, puts behind them the force of tradition and precept, and organizes the mighty sanction of human disapproval. Thus, he conceives that Masonry is working hand in hand with church and state, in organizing the conditions of social progress; and that all societies and organizations, local or cosmopolitan, which seek to unify men's energies in any sphere-- whether science, or art, or labor, or commerce --have their part also; since each and all, held up by the three pillars of the social order--Religion, Law, and Morals; Wisdom, Strength, and Beauty--are making for human perfection.

But, in the attainment of human perfection, we must go beyond the strict limits of the social order. Morality, as we have seen, is an institution of social man. Nevertheless it has possibilities of its own, surpassing the essential requirements of a society. There is a moral order, above and developed out of the social t order, as the social order is above the natural. The natural order is maintained by the instincts of self and species preservation. These instincts, unrestrained, take no account of other existences, and make struggle for existence the rule.

In the social order, men have learned to adjust act to end in maintaining their own lives without hindering others from doing the like. In the moral order, men have learned not merely to live without hindering the lives of others, but to live so as to aid others in attaining a more complete and perfect life. When the life of every individual is full and complete, not merely without hindering other lives from like completeness, but while helping them to attain it, perfection will have been reached. Then will the individual, "In hand and foot and soul four-square, fashioned without fault," fit closely into the moral order, as the perfect ashlar. Instinct maintains the natural order. Law must stand chiefly behind the social order. Masonry will find its sphere, for the most part, in maintaining and developing the moral order. So that, while it reminds us of our natural duties to ourselves, and of the duties we owe our country, as the embodiment of the social order, it insists, above and beyond them all, upon our duties to our neighbor and to God, through which alone the perfection of the moral order may be attained.

Krause does not believe, however, that law and the state should limit their scope and purpose to keeping up the social order. They maintain right and justice in order to uphold society. But they uphold society in order to liberate men's energies so that they may make for the moral order. Hence the ultimate aim is human perfection. If by any act intended to maintain the social order, they retard the moral order, they are going counter to their ends. Law and morals are distinct; but their aim is one, and the distinction is in the fields in which they may act effectively and in the means of action, rather than in the ideas themselves. The lawgiver must never forget the ultimate purpose, and must seek to advance rather than to hinder the organization and harmonious development of all human activities. "Law," he tells us, "is the sum of the external conditions of life measured by reason." So far as perfection may be reached by limitation of the external acts of men, whereby each may live a complete life, unhindered by his fellows, the law is effective. More than this, the external conditions of the life measured by reason are, indirectly, conditions of the fuller and completer life of the moral order; for men must be free to exercise their best energies without hindrance, before they can employ them to much purpose in aiding others to a larger life. Here, however, law exhausts its possibilities. It upholds the social order, whereon the moral order rests. The development and maintenance of the moral order depend on internal conditions. And these are without the domain of law. Nevertheless, as law prepares the way for the moral order, morals make more easy the task of law. The more thoroughly each individual, of his own motion, measures his life by reason, the more completely does law cease to be merely regulative and restraining, and attains its higher role of an organized human freedom. Here is one of the prime functions of the symbols of the Craft. As one reflects upon these symbols, the idea of life measured by reason is everywhere borne in upon him. The twenty-four inch gauge, the plumb, the level, the square and compass, and the trestle board are eloquent of measurement and restraint.

There is nothing measured in the life of the savage. He may kill sufficient for his needs, or, from mere caprice or wanton love of slaughter, may kill beyond his needs at the risk of future want. His acts have little or no relation to one another. He does not sow at one season that he may reap at another, much less does he plant or build in one generation that another generation may be nourished or sheltered. The exigencies or the desires of the moment control his actions. On the other hand, the acts of civilized man are connected, related to one another, and, to a great extent, parts of a harmonious and intelligent scheme of activity. Even more is this true of conduct which is called moral. Its prime characteristic is certainty. We know today what it will be tomorrow. The unprincipled may or may not keep promises, may or may not pay debts, may or may not be constant in political or family relations. The man whose conduct is moral, we call trustworthy. We repose entire confidence in his steadfast adherence to a regular and orderly course of life. Hence we speak of rectitude of conduct, under the figure of adjustment to a straight line; and our whole nomenclature of ethics is based upon such figures of speech. Excess, which is indefinite and unmeasured, is immoral; moderation, which implies adherence to a definite and ascertainable medium, we feel to be moral. The social man, as distinguished from the savage, and even more the moral man, as distinguished from him who merely takes care not to infringe the law, measures and lays out his life, and the symbols of the Craft serve as continual monitors to the weak or thoughtless of what must distinguish them from the savage and the unprincipled.

The allegory of the house not built with hands, into which we are to be fitted as living stones, suggests reflections still more inspiring. Here we see symbolized the organic conception of society and of human activities, upon which Krause insists so strongly. Social and individual progress, he says, are inseparable. Nothing is to be kept back or hindered in the march toward human perfection. The social order conserves the end of self and race maintenance more perfectly than the natural order, which aims at nothing higher; and the moral order accomplishes the end of maintaining society more fully than a system that attempts no more. The complete life is a complete life of the units, as well as of the whole, and the progress of humanity is a harmonizing of the interests of each with each other and with all. Nature is wasteful. Myriads of seeds are produced that a few plants may struggle to maturity. Multitudes of lives are lost in the struggle for existence, that a few may survive. As men advance in social and moral development, this sacrifice of individuals becomes continually less. The most perfect state, in consequence, is that in which the welfare of each citizen and that of all citizens have become identical, where the interests of state and subject are one, where the feelings of each accord with those of all. In this era of universal organization, when Krause's chapters seem almost prophetic, there is much to console us in his belief that the organic must prove harmonious, and that organizations which now conflict will in the end work consciously and unerringly, as they now work unconsciously and imperfectly, toward a common end. If, as his illustrious pupil tells us, "human society is but a solid bundle of organic institutions, a federation of particular organizations, through which the fundamental aims of humanity are realized," we may confidently hope for unity where now is discord. And we may hope for most of all, in this work of unification, from that world-wide Brotherhood, which has for its mission to organize morals and to bring them home as realities to every man.

To sum up, how does Krause answer the three problems of Masonic philosophy ?

1) What is the purpose for which Masonry exists? What does it seek to do? Krause answers that in common with all other human institutions its ultimate purpose is the perfection of humanity. But its immediate purpose is to organize the universal moral sentiments of mankind; to organize the sanction of human disapproval.

2) What is the relation of Masonry to other human institutions, especially to government and religion, state and church? Krause answers that these aim also at human perfection. Immediately each seeks to organize some particular branch of human

activity. But they do this as means to a common end. Hence, he says, each of these organizations should work in harmony and even in co-operation with the others toward the great end of all of them. In this spirit expounds the well-known exhortations in our charges with respect to the attitude of the Mason toward the government and the religion of his country.

3) What are the fundamental principles by which Masonry is governed in attaining the end it seeks? Krause answers: Masonry has to deal with the internal conditions of life governed by reason. Hence its fundamental principles are measurement and restraint-- measurement by reason and restraint by reason--and it teaches these as a means of achieving perfection.

Such, in brief and meager outline, is the relation of Masonry to the philosophy of law and government, as conceived by one who has left his mark on the history of each. Think what we may of some of his doctrines, differ with him as we may at many points, hold, as we may, that our Order has other ends, we must needs be stirred by the noble aim he has set before us; we must needs be animated by a higher spirit and more strenuous purpose, as one of the chiefest of the organic societies composing the "solid bundle" that makes for human perfection.

PART III
OLIVER

Krause's philosophy is concerned chiefly with the relation of Masonry to the philosophy of law and government. Oliver's philosophy of Masonry deals rather with Masonry in its relation to the philosophy of religion. In order to understand this we need only note that Krause was by profession a philosopher and that the main work of his life was done in the philosophy of law and of government while, on the other hand, Oliver was a clergyman. As in Preston's case, Oliver's general philosophical ideas came to him ready-made. He flowed with the philosophical current of his time. He did not turn it into new channels or affect its course as did Krause. Hence here, as with Preston, we may conveniently consider Oliver's philosophy of Masonry under three heads:

1) The man
2) The time
3) His Masonic philosophy as a product of the two.

The man. George Oliver was born at Pepplewick in the county of Nottingham, November 5, 1782. His father was a clergyman of the established church and his mother was the daughter of a country gentleman. Hence he had the advantage of a bringing up under conditions of culture and refinement. He was educated at Nottingham and made such progress that at twenty-one he was made second master of the grammar school at Caistor in Lincolnshire. Six years later he was made head master of King Edward's grammar school at Great Grimsby. In 1813 he took orders but continued to teach. In 1815 he was given a living by his bishop as the result of an examination and at the same time, as the phrase was, was put on the boards of Trinity College, Cambridge, as a so-called ten-year man. That is he was given ten years in which to earn his degree. Thus in 1836 he was able to take his degree of doctor of divinity. In the meantime he was successively promoted to parishes of more and more importance till he became rector of Wolverhampton and prebendary of the collegiate church. In 1846 the lord chancellor gave him an easier and more lucrative living. He died in 1866 at the age of eighty four.

Beginning in 1811 Oliver was a diligent student of and a prolific writer upon antiquities, particularly ecclesiastical antiquities and his writings soon brought him a high reputation as an antiquary. It is worth while to give a list of the more important of these books since taken in connection with the long list of his Masonic writings it will afford some idea of his diligence and activity. I give only those which have been considered the more important.

1) History and Antiquities of the Collegiate Church of Beverley.
2) History and Antiquities of the Collegiate Church of Wolverhampton.
3) History of the Conventual Church of Grimsby.
4) Monumental Antiquities of Grimsby.

5) History of the Guild of the Holy Trinity, Sleaford.
6) Druidical Remains near Lincoln.
7) Guide to the Druidical Temple at Nottingham.
8) Remains of the Ancient Britons between Lincoln and Sleaford.

To these must be added a great mass of papers and notes on antiquarian matters published between 1811 and 1866. And be it remembered the author was, while most of these were writing, a teacher studying during his leisure hours in preparation for orders and later for his degree and when the remainder were written was rector of an important parish, a magistrate, a surrogate for the bishopric of Lincoln and a steward of the clerical fund for his diocese. This sounds like one man's work and a good measure at that. To it, however, we have to add a Masonic literary career even more fruitful and more enduring in its results.

Oliver was made a Mason at the age of nineteen. This statement, startling to the modern Masonic ear, requires explanation. As Masonic usage then stood a "lewis," that is the son of a Mason, might be initiated by dispensation before he came of age. The privileges of a lewis have never been defined clearly. He was supposed to have a right of initiation in precedence over all other candidates. Also in England and France he was supposed to have the right to be initiated at an earlier age, namely eighteen. The constitutions are silent on this point but the traditional custom was to grant a dispensation in the case of a lewis after that age. It is hard to say how far this usage has ever obtained in America. At present it is not recognized. But there is evidence that it obtained in the eighteenth century as, for example, in the case of George Washington who was initiated at the age of twenty. At any rate Oliver became a Mason in this way at the age of nineteen being initiated by his father in St. Peters Lodge at Peterborough in 1801.

Oliver's father was a zealous and well-informed Mason and a ritualist of the literal school, that is of the type who regard literal expertness in ritual as the unum necessarium in Masonry. Accordingly Oliver was thoroughly trained on this side--which indeed is indispensable not only to Masonic advancement but, I suspect, to Masonic scholarship--and as a result of his thorough knowledge of the work and his tireless activity his rise in the Craft was rapid.

In 1809 Oliver established a lodge at Grimsby where he was the master of the grammar school and chiefly by his exertions the lodge became strong and prosperous. He was master of that lodge fourteen years. Thence successively he became Provincial Grand Steward (1813); Grand Chaplain (1816); and Deputy Grand Master of Lincolnshire (1832). The latter office he held for eight years. It should be remembered that the post of Provincial Grand Master was reserved in England for the nobility. It is interesting to know in passing that the Grand Lodge of Massachusetts gave him the honorary title of Past

Deputy Grand Master.

The list of Oliver's Masonic writings is very long. He is the most prolific of Masonic authors and on the whole has had the widest influence. He began by publishing a number of Masonic sermons but presently as one may suspect by way of revolt from the mechanical ritualistic Masonry to which, as it were, he had been bred he turned his attention to the history and subsequently to the philosophy of the Craft.

His first historical work is the well-known:

1) Antiquities of Free Masonry: comprising illustrations of the five grand periods of Masonry from the creation of the world to the dedication of King Solomon's temple. This was published in 1823.

Then followed in order:

2) The Star in the East, his first philosophical work, designed to show the relation of Masonry to religion.

3) Signs and Symbols, an exposition of the history and significance of all the Masonic symbols then recognized.

4) History of Initiation, twelve lectures on the ancient mysteries in which Oliver sought to trace Masonic initiation and ancient systems of initiation to a common origin; a matter with respect to which recent anthropological and sociological studies of primitive secret societies indicate that he may have hit the truth much more nearly than we had been supposing of late.

5) The Theocratic Philosophy of Masonry, a

further development of his ideas as to the relation of Masonry to religion.

6) A History of Free Masonry from 1829 to 1840, intended as an appendix to Preston's Illustrations of Masonry which he had edited in 1829.

7) Historical Landmarks and Other Evidences of Masonry Explained, by far his greatest work, a monument of wide reading and laborious research.

8) Revelations of a Square, a bit of Masonic fiction.

9) The Golden Remains of the Early Masonic Writers, an elaborate compilation in five volumes.

10) The Symbol of Glory, his best discussion of the object and purpose of Masonry.

11) A Mirror for the Johannite Masons, in which he discusses the dedication of lodges and the two Sts. John.

12) The Origin and Insignia of the Royal Arch Degree.

13) A Dictionary of Symbolic Masonry, the first of a long line of such dictionaries.

14) Institutes of Masonic Jurisprudence.

He also published a "Book of the Lodge," a sort of ritualistic manual similar to the monitors or manuals so well known today. Likewise he was a constant contributor to English and even to American Masonic periodicals.

Probably no one not by profession a writer can show such a list, bearing in mind how many of the foregoing are books of the first order in their class.

Unhappily Oliver's views of Masonic law were

not in accord with those which prevailed in England in 1840. In consequence when in that year Dr. Crucefix, one of the most distinguished of nineteenth-century English Masons, was suspended by the Grand Lodge and retired from Masonic activity Oliver also incurred the displeasure of the authorities by claiming the right, though a Provincial Deputy Grand Master, to take part in a public demonstration in honor of Crucefix in which a large number of prominent Masons joined. This led to his losing his office by the action of the Provincial Grand Master and to his withdrawing from active connection with the Craft. But English Masons soon came to see the soundness of Oliver's views as to the independence which Masonry must allow to the individual in his belief and opinion as to what is Masonic law. Accordingly four years later nearly all the Masons in the kingdom joined in subscribing for a presentation of plate to Oliver in recognition of his great services to the Craft. But justice was not done to Oliver as it was to Preston possibly because Oliver was not the type of man to urge it for himself as Preston would have done. In consequence Oliver was out of touch with active Masonic work for the last twenty two years of his life. That this was in no way due to improper obstinacy on his part is, I think, manifest from merely looking at his portrait--which radiates benevolence and amiability. Moreover all accounts of his personality agree with the impression one gets from the portrait. All accounts bear witness to his lovableness, his geniality, his charitableness and his readiness to oblige. All who have written of him testify that he was in the highest degree unassuming, unaffected and easy of approach. That such men as Krause and Oliver should suffer from the jealousies which greater knowledge seems to engender in those who regard ability to recite the ritual with microscopic fidelity as the sum of Masonry is not wholly to be wondered at. The breadth which such knowledge inevitably brings about threatens the very foundations of the literalism which the strongest men in our lodges have been taught or have taught themselves is the essence of the institution. But it is strange and is an unhappy commentary upon human nature that the arrogant, ambitious Preston could at length obtain justice which was denied to Krause and to Oliver.

Summing up Oliver's personality, everything confirms the impression which one derives from the portrait. He was a warm-hearted man, of zealous antiquarian enthusiasm, of deep faith and of thoroughgoing religious convictions. We must remember each of these traits when we come to consider his philosophy of Masonry. So much for the man.

Now for the time.

The dominant philosophy everywhere when Oliver wrote was what is known as romanticism. In England, which at this period was still primarily taken up with religious rather than with philosophical or scientific questions, romanticism was especially strong. Thinkers of the generation after Kant objected to his critical philosophy on the ground that it lacked vitality. They asserted that the living unity of the spirit was violated by his analyzings and distinguishings. They pointed to religious faith on the one hand and to artistic conception and creation on the other hand as methods which unlike the critical philosophy did full justice to life. In other words the age of reason in which Preston wrought and wrote was over and for a season at least men ceased to expect all things of reason, intellect and knowledge and began to expect all things of what they called spirit. The younger thinkers especially were filled with enthusiasm at this idea of deducing all things from spirit and did not see that they were simply seeking for a new philosopher's stone. They expected through the idea of the spirit to establish a complete unity of all things, to break down the existing separation between science, religion and art and to reconcile all discords. Such an idea of knowledge rightly may be called romantic. It stands before us sublime and distant. It rouses our enthusiasm or our zeal to achieve it, and influences us by its exaltation rather than by any prospect which it affords us of clear and sober realization. That a whole generation should have been content to put its ideal of knowledge in this form seems difficult to explain even by reaction from the over-rationalism of the preceding century. Probably the general upheaval brought about by the French Revolution must be taken into account and the golden age of poetry which accompanied this philosophical movement must not be overlooked. Indeed the connection between the romantic philosophers, the romantic poets and the romantic musicians is very close. It is not an accident that what I may fairly call romantic Masonry appears at the same time. This will be manifest especially when I come to speak of Oliver's views as to the relation of Masonry to religion.

One of the most representative of the German romantic philosophers argued that all separation between poetry, philosophy and religion was superficial and arbitrary. He argued that while the poet regards philosophy as an expounding of the poetry of life which is to be found in all things, the philosopher regards poetry as a pictorial form, perceived intuitively, of the thought which moves in all things. But, he said, religion is a phase of the same quest for unity. Let me quote his words since they bear strongly upon Oliver's views: "If it is allowed that the task of thought is to show us the unity of all things, can philosophical endeavor differ in its essence from the religious yearning which likewise seeks to transcend the oppositions and unrest of life ?"

This romantic philosophy came into England chiefly through the poet Samuel Taylor Coleridge (1772-1834) who wrote while Oliver's chief literary activities were in progress and died about six years before the most important and significant of Oliver's writings. The relation of the one to the other is so clear that a moment's digression as to Coleridge is necessary.

In his youth Coleridge tells us he had been a

disciple of the eighteenth-century rationalists. But he was repelled by the attempt, so characteristic of the eighteenth century, to reduce mental phenomena to elementary functions by means of analysis and to discover mechanical laws for all consciousness. If this could be done, he said, it would destroy the unity and activity of the mind. At this time he came in contact with the German romantic philosophy and turned in the new direction. Indeed he was a romanticist by nature. He reveled, it has been said, in ideas of the absolute in which the differences and oppositions of the finite world blended and disappeared. He was a poet and a preacher rather than a thinker and rarely got beyond intuition and prophecy. Hence there is more than a little truth in the saying of one of his critics that he led his generation through moonshine to orthodoxy and to a more pronounced orthodoxy than had formerly obtained. It is said that the Anglo-Catholic or Puseyite movement of the nineteenth century, which carried Newman and so many other English scholars into the church of Rome, was a result of Coleridge's ideas.

What, then, were the characteristics of the philosophy of the time and place in which Oliver wrote?

1) Speculation and imagination were the chief organs of thought. The poetic passed for the only real. Enthusiasm passed for scholarship.

2) Reason abdicated for a season. Conviction, intuition and faith were regarded as justifying them-

selves.

3) In the same way tradition became something which justified itself. This is seen particularly in the so-called Oxford movement and the Catholic reaction in England. It is seen also in the position of the time as to the English constitution which Dickens has satirized in the person of Mr. Podsnap.

4) Reconciliation of Christianity with philosophy became a recognized problem. For example, Coleridge took this for his chief work.

All of these features may be seen in Oliver's Masonic writings. The defects of his historical writing, for example, which have utterly debased popular Masonic history are the defects of a romanticist. A warm imagination and speculative enthusiasm carried him away. In common with his philosophical teachers he had thrown off the critical method and had lost the faculty of discriminating accurately between what had been and what he would like to believe had been. On the other hand, in Masonic philosophy, where pure speculation was allowable, these qualities had a certain value. Mill says of Coleridge that his was one of the great seminal minds of his time. In the same way Oliver more than anyone else set men to thinking upon the problems of Masonic philosophy. His style is agreeable. He is always easy to read and often entertaining. A multitude of readers, who would be repelled by Krause's learned but difficult pages, have rejoiced in Oliver. Hence he has given a form and direction to Masonic speculation which still persist.

Turning to Oliver's philosophy of Masonry three important points may be noted:

1) His theory of the relation of Masonry to religion

2) His theory of Masonry as a tradition coming down to us from a pure state prior to the flood

3) His theory of the essentially Christian nature of our institution.

Let me take these up in order.

1) It has been said that reconciliation of knowledge with religion and unifying of religion with all other human activities was a favorite undertaking of the romantic philosophy. It was natural, therefore that a clergyman should be attracted to this type of thought and that a zealous churchman and enthusiastic Mason who had learned from Preston, whose book he edited, that Masonry was knowledge, should convert the problem into one of relating Masonry to religion and of reconciling them. Oliver's mode of doing this was highly ingenious. Religion and Masonry, he would say, are identical in their end and they are identical in their end with knowledge. Each is a manifestation of the spirit, the absolute, that is of God. God, he would say, is manifest to us, first, by revelation and thus manifest we know Him and know ourselves and know the universe through religion. Second, He is manifest to us by tradition, and in this way we know Him and know ourselves and know the universe through Masonry. Third, He is manifest to us through reason, and in this way we know Him and

know ourselves and know the universe through knowledge or, as we have come to call it, science. In common with the romanticists he sought to throw the entire content of life into one interconnected whole; and this he found in God or in the absolute. Accordingly to him Masonry was one mode of approach to God, the other two being religion and science. If Krause's triad was law, religion, morals, given effect by state, church, Masonry, Oliver's is revelation, tradition, reason, expounded, handed down, developed and interpreted by religion, Masonry and science.

    2) Oliver's theory of Masonry as a system of tradition seems to have been derived from Hutchinson. The latter deserves a moment's digression.

    William Hutchinson (1732-1814), an English lawyer, is perhaps the earliest Masonic philosopher. In 1774 by permission of the Grand Lodge, which then insisted upon a right to censor all Masonic writing, Hutchinson published his chief Masonic work entitled "The Spirit of Masonry." Oliver himself has said that this book was "the first efficient attempt to explain in a rational and scientific manner the true philosophy of the order." Hutchinson's doctrine was that the lost word was symbolical of lost religious purity due to corruptions of the Jewish faith. He held that the master's degree symbolized the new law of Christ taking the place of the old law of Judaism which had become dead and corrupt. By a bit of fanciful etymologer he derived Hiram (Huram) from the Greek heuramen (we have found it) and Acacia from the Greek alpha privative and Kakia (evil)--Akakia, freedom from evil, or freedom from sin. Thus, he says, the Master Mason "represents a man under the Christian doctrine saved from the grave of iniquity and raised to the faith of salvation." Hutchinson influenced Hemming, who wrote the lectures of the Ancients and a trace of this influence may be seen in America in the interpretation of the blazing star in our lectures.

Clearly enough Oliver got his cue from Hutchinson. But Hutchinson had identified religion and Masonry. This Oliver, as a clergyman of the established church, could not allow. Instead Oliver sought to unify them, that is while keeping them distinct to make them phases of a higher unity, to make them expressions of what is ultimately, though not immediately, one. This he did as has been seen by regarding each as a mode of approach to God. That conception led to his theory of Masonry as a body of tradition.

Briefly stated Oliver's theory is this. He held that Masonry was to be found as a body of tradition in the earliest periods of history as recorded in Scripture. This tradition according to his enthusiastic speculations was taught by Seth to his descendants and was practiced by them as a pure or primitive Masonry before the flood. Thus it passed over to Noah and his descendants and at the dispersion of mankind was divided into pure Masonry and spurious Masonry. The pure Masonry passed through the patriarchs to Solomon and thence to the present institution. On the other hand, the pure tradition was corrupted among the pagans and took the form of the mysteries and initiatory rites of antiquity. Accordingly, he held, we have in Masonry a traditional science of morality veiled in allegory and illustrated by symbols.

3) Again taking his cue from Hutchinson, though the old charges to be true to holy church gave him some warrant--Oliver insisted that Masonry was strictly a Christian institution. He believed of course that Christianity was foretold and in a way revealed in the Old Testament and that the doctrine of the Trinity, for example, was clearly expounded therein. In the same way he held that the earliest of Masonic symbols also taught the doctrine of the Trinity and that the Masonic references to the Grand Architect of the Universe were references to Christ. Indeed in his system this was necessary. For if religion, which to him could mean only the Christian religion, and Masonry were to be unified it must be as setting before us different manifestations of the same God. There could be but one God and that triune God, the God of his religion, he held was made known to us by revelation, by tradition and by reason. Thus Oliver's interpretation of revelation determined his interpretation of the other two. If we bear this in mind we may accept his general philosophy without accepting this particular doctrine. For it needs only to postulate a more universal and more general religion than he professed, a religion above sects, creeds and dogmas to hold that such a religion along with

Masonry and along with reason leads to God. Moreover Hindu and Mohammedan may each put his own interpretation on revelation and join in believing in these three modes of knowing the absolute. Mackey reproaches Oliver for narrowness and sectarianism. But the possibilities of his Masonic philosophy are as broad as could be desired. It was too soon in 1840 to ask a clergyman to go further in its application than he went.

What then are Oliver's answers to the three fundamental questions of Masonic philosophy?

1) What is the end of Masonry, for what does the institution exist? Oliver would answer, it is one in its end with religion and with science. Each of these are means through which we are brought into relation with the absolute. They are the means through which we know God and his works.

2) How does Masonry seek to achieve its end? Oliver would answer by preserving, handing down and interpreting a tradition of immemorial antiquity, a pure tradition from the childhood of the race.

3) What are the fundamental principles by which Masonry is governed in achieving its task? Oliver would say, the fundamental principles of Masonry are essentially the principles of religion as the basic principles of the moral world. But in Masonry they appear in a traditional form. Thus, for example, toleration in Masonry is a form of what in religion we call charity; universality in Masonry is a traditional form of what in religion we call love of one's neighbor.

As has been said, Krause's was a philosophy of Masonry in its relation to law and government. Preston's was a philosophy of Masonry in its relation to knowledge. Oliver's is a philosophy of Masonry in its relation to religion. Neither of the others has had a tithe of the influence which Oliver's philosophy has exerted upon Masonic thought. And on the whole his influence has been valuable and stimulating. A critic has said that "all he had to give was transcendental moonshine which shed a new light on old things for many a young doubter and seeker, but which contained no new life." In a sense this is so. Oliver's Masonic philosophy is an obvious product of a clergyman in the age of the romantic philosophy who had read and reflected upon Hutchinson. And yet it is not true that there is no new life in Oliver. Except for Krause nothing so well worth while has been pointed out for Masonry as the end which Oliver found for us. I cannot but feel that it is a great misfortune that his philosophy is being peddled out to a new generation in grandiloquent fragments through Grand Lodge orations and articles in the Masonic press instead of being apprehended as a whole.

PART IV
PIKE

We come now to a radically different type of Masonic philosophy. To Preston Masonry is a traditional system of knowledge and its end is to impart knowledge. Hence he thinks of the relation of Masonry to education. To Krause it is organized morals and its end is to put organized mankind behind the universal moral ideas of humanity. Hence he thinks of the relation of Masonry to law and government. To Oliver it is a mode of approach to God and its end is to bring us to the Absolute by means of a pure tradition. Hence he thinks of the relation of Masonry to religion. Pike gives us instead a metaphysic of Masonry. To him Masonry is a mode of studying first principles and its end is to reveal and to give us possession of the universal principle by which we may master the universe. Hence he thinks of the relation of Masonry to the fundamental problems of existence. In part this view was inevitable in one who thought and wrote in a country under the influence of the transcendental philosophy. In part also it was to be expected in a member of a profession whose philosophical ideas, so far as its leaders held any at all, were thoroughly Hegelian. In part it grew out of Pike's wide reading in the philosophical writings of antiquity and his bent for mysticism. Thus his philosophy of Masonry is a product of the man and of the time and we must look first at each of these in order to treat it intelligently.

1) The man. Albert Pike was born in Boston, December 29, 1809. His parents were poor. He was educated in the public schools in Boston and it is interesting to know as a means of comparing those days with these that, although he passed the examinations for admission to Harvard College, he was unable to enter because in those days the requirement was that two years' tuition be paid in advance or secured by bond. He became a school teacher and taught in country schools in Massachusetts from 1825 to 1831. In 1831 he went west and joined a trading party from St. Louis to Santa Fe. Santa Fe was then in Mexico and the journey at that time was a perilous one through a wilderness inhabited only by Indians. On his, return he traversed the Staked Plains and the Indian Territory and settled finally at Van Buren in Arkansas where he opened a school.

At that time political feeling in Arkansas was very bitter. The territory was divided between the Conway party who were politically democrats and in truth were a sort of clan as well, and the Crittenden party who were Whigs politically but were in truth more a personal faction than a political party. Bloodshed was frequent and in many respects there was a feud between the factions quite as much as a political rivalry. The early experience of this era of feud and private war on the frontier is worth remembering in connection with many things in Pike's lectures upon Masonry. Pike was a Whig and as such published in the Whig organ at Little Rock some articles of such force as to attract general attention. Accordingly

Crittend, the Whig leader, sought out Pike in his country school-room and induced him to go to Little Rock as one of the editors of the party organ. This was his opportunity and he improved it to the full by studying law while, also at work upon the paper. In 1834 he was admitted to the bar and he rose rapidly to the first rank in the profession in Arkansas. Among his earlier achievements was the preparation of the first revision of the statutes of that state. The book does not bear his name but contemporary accounts tell us that he had the chief part in framing it. By general consent it is a model of what such a work should be.

At the outbreak of the Mexican war Pike entered the service and was in action at Buena Vista. His courage, proved already in the political conflicts of territorial days, was again shown in events that grew out of the campaign in Mexico. Pike felt it his duty to criticize the military conduct of Governor Roane and as a result was compelled to fight a duel. The duel took place over the line in the Indian Territory. Happily it was bloodless and ended in reconciliation. There is good reason to suspect that some traces of this experience are to be seen in his lectures.

From 1853 to 1857 Pike practiced law in New Orleans. Thus he was led to make a diligent and characteristically thorough study of Roman law, the basis of the French law which obtained then, as it does now, in Louisiana. In 1857 he returned to Arkansas and afterward sat upon the supreme bench of that state. At the outbreak of the Civil War he cast his lot with the South. As he had great influence with the Indians he was sent to raise a force in the Indian Territory. In this work he was vigorous and untiring. But his utmost efforts could not make obedient or efficient soldiers out of the large force which he was able to raise. Some of the doings of this force have left a stain upon his memory, which, according to the best authorities obtainable, seems to be undeserved. In truth his experience was not very different from that of the British officers during the Revolution and during the War of 1812 who sought to make military use of Indian allies. In any event the project failed. This experience also has left more than one trace in his Masonic lectures. After the Civil War he practiced law for a time in Memphis. In 1868 he went to Alexandria, Virginia, and in 1870 moved across the river to Washington where he practiced law for twenty-one years. He died in 1891.

Albert Pike was a man of the widest and most varied learning. He was a strong and successful common-law lawyer. He had studied the Roman law to good purpose and left a manuscript of a three-volume book upon the principles of the Roman law which is now in the library of the Supreme Court of the United states. But he had many scholarly interests outside of his profession. He left among his papers a manuscript translation of the Zend Avesta and of the Rig Veda in twenty-two large volumes copiously annotated. Moreover he made some mark as a poet. Some of his poems, particularly a striking one upon the battle of Buena Vista, are still to be found in school readers and his verses were formerly much in vogue. Reviewing his extra-Masonic record for a moment, we see a man born and educated in New England, a pioneer in the southwest in its frontier period, a soldier in two wars, a successful lawyer under each of the two great systems of modern law, for a season judge of a supreme court and withal, though largely self-educated, a man of learning and culture who, along with a treatise upon the principles of Roman law which bore immediately upon his profession, could write verse of some merit and could busy himself in the translation of the great books of Oriental philosophy and religion.

But the field of Pike's most fruitful labors was Masonry. His career as a Mason is too recent and his standing as a Masonic scholar is too well-known to all of you to call for any statement in this place. But I may remind you that he became Sovereign Grand Commander of the southern jurisdiction in the Scottish Rite in 1859 and devoted the remaining thirty-two years of his life in continually increasing measure to the work of that rite. Excepting Krause no mind of equal caliber has been employed upon the problems of Masonry. And Krause, great scholar and philosopher as he was, had lived only in the cultured serenity of German university towns whereas Pike had lived in staid Boston and turbulent territorial Arkansas, had been compelled by local public opinion to fight in a duel, had fought in two wars and had commanded Indians. Moreover, Krause's Masonic experience was negligible in comparison with that of this veteran of American Masonry. Accordingly we need not hesitate to pronounce Albert Pike by far the best qualified by nature, experience of life, Masonic experience and Masonic learning of those who have thought upon the problems of Masonic philosophy.

2) Now as to the time.

In the earlier part of his career, Pike was brought into contact with the eighteenth-century political philosophy which became classical in American political thought because it was the philosophy of the framers of our constitutions and bills of rights and entered into the framework of our institutions in their formative period. Also in this part of his career, in his study of law, he came in contact with the eighteenth-century legal philosophy of the American common-law lawyer. In the latter part of his career, in his wide philosophical studies, he was brought into contact with the prevailing metaphysical method of the nineteenth century, with the conception of the Absolute, which governed in English philosophical writing, and with the method of unifying all things by reference to some basic absolute principle which prevailed down to the new century. This same period saw the general rise of materialism in the wake of decay of dogma and the triumphant advance of the natural sciences, and this movement so far affected his thought as to turn him, by way of reaction, to mysticism. Indeed a mystic element is to be found not uncommonly in thorough-going idealists. For example the leader of the new school that builds on

Hegel's philosophy has been reproved for dragging mysticism into so prosaic a subject as the philosophy of law. But mystics are made by nature, and nature made Pike one of the greatest of them. Hence we may be confident that reaction from materialism merely accentuated an element which in any event would have been prominent in his thinking and writing. Each of the four points of contact with American thought in the nineteenth century requires a moment's consideration.

American political philosophy in the first half of the nineteenth century was a compound of English law and French speculation. Prior to the Revolution in the Declaration of Rights of the Continental Congress the colonists had relied upon the common-law rights of Englishmen as asserted by English lawyers and English judges against the Stuart kings in the seventeenth century. But the Declaration of Independence relied instead upon the natural rights of man, a supposed body of universal, eternal, inalienable rights deduced by reason from the nature of man in the abstract. Under the influence of English thinkers of the seventeenth century and of the Continental philosophy of law in the period after Grotius, the French writers of the eighteenth century had developed this theory of natural rights to a high degree, and the founders of our government were deeply read in their writings. But they were also deeply read in Blackstone and in Coke, the oracle of English law. Naturally they combined the general theory of the French speculators and the concrete details of the

English lawyers and came to hold that the common-law rights of Englishmen found in their law books were the natural rights of man found in their French political philosophy. Hence in our bills of rights they laid down the former section by section and enacted them in fixed and precise rules on the authority of the latter. This had important consequences for the American legal philosophy which Pike absorbed in the formative period of his study for the bar.

In the contests between the English judges and the Stuart kings the judges had claimed to stand between the rights and liberties of the individual Englishman and arbitrary oppressive action on the part of the crown. When we took over the theory of eternal, inalienable natural rights and combined it with the theory of the English lawyers, the result was a doctrine that law stands and must stand between the individual on the one hand and state and society on the other hand and that its function is to secure the individual in his natural rights against the aggressions and oppressions of organized society. This idea of the mediating function of law, as a reconciling of the individual and the whole, which the lawyer of the last century took for the first article of his creed, is to be seen throughout Pike's lectures and lent itself readily to his generalization of equilibrium or balance as the Ultimate Reality. For if law was a mediation, a harmonizing, a reconciling, and the universe was governed by law, the fundamental principle of the universe was the mediating or harmonizing which he called equilibrium.

When, in his later studies, Pike came upon the metaphysical method of nineteenth-century philosophers, it was easy to confirm the views to which his acquaintance with the classical American political and legal philosophy and his reading of French Masonic writers of the eighteenth century had led him. For the generation that followed Hegel sought to explain the universe as the realization of an idea. History was the unfolding of that idea in human experience. Philosophy was a logical unfolding of the same idea. Hence the quest was for the one fundamental idea of which the seemingly complex order of the phenomenal world was but a manifestation. Hence the task of the philosopher was to unite and reconcile all differences in the Absolute which he reached through this idea. Traces of the transition from the legal and political analogy to this metaphysical foundation may be seen here and there in those parts of Morals and Dogma which, we may suspect, remained in their earlier forms despite his repeated and thorough-going revisions.

In his later studies Pike was also compelled to take account of the materialism which held its head so high and with "a mouth speaking great things" grew so confidently dogmatic during the last third of his life. If Pike, who was naturally a mystic, seems sometimes to rely on intuition more than on reason, to put faith, which is self-justifying, at the bottom of knowledge, to find a reality in the occult, and to show a conviction of the relation of the symbol to the thing symbolized, in contrast with the rigorous metaphysic of the lectures where he argues and demonstrates instead of prophesying, we must consider the impatience of an idealist and a mystic with the mechanical universe of the positivists and the economic ethics and belly-philosophy of the materialists which a new generation was asserting all about him.

3) Let us turn now to Pike's Masonic philosophy. Pike did not leave us any compendium of his philosophical views. Hence we cannot, as in the case of Oliver, apprehend them at a glance from a concise exposition. The student of Pike's Masonic philosophy must read and study the teeming pages of Morals and Dogma. After reading and reflection the system of philosophy expounded will make itself felt. But it is quite impossible for the reader to put his finger upon this sentence or that and say here is Pike's philosophy in a nut-shell. For the first thing to bear in mind in reading Morals and Dogma is that we must discriminate closely between what is really Pike and what is not.

Indeed he has told us this himself.

"In preparing this work, the Grand Commander has been about equally Author and Compiler; since he has extracted quite half its contents from the works of the best writers and most philosophic or eloquent thinkers. Perhaps it would have been better and more acceptable, if he had extracted more and written less.

"Still, perhaps half of it is his own; and, in incorporating here the thoughts and words of others, he has continually changed and added to the language, often intermingling, in the same sentences, his own words with theirs."

In some measure the author is unjust to himself in this statement. In a sense the book is all his own. He read and digested everything. He assimilated it. He made it part of himself and worked it into his system. But for this very reason texts from Pike and excepts from Morals and Dogma are more than usually deceptive. We may fasten almost any philosophical idea upon him if we proceed in this way. We may refute almost any page by any other page if we look simply at the surface and do not distinguish matter which he is adapting or is making use of to illustrate the development of thought upon the subject from dogmatic statements of his philosophy. Morals and Dogma must be read and interpreted as a unit. As Immanuel Kant said of his own writings, it is a book to think through not merely to read through.

Three contributions of the first moment to Masonic science deserve to be noted before taking up Pike's philosophy of Masonry in detail. In the first place Pike was the apostle of liberty of interpretation. He insisted in season and out of season that no infallible authority speaking ex cathedra could bind the individual Mason to this or that interpretation of the traditional symbols of the Craft. He taught that the individual Mason instead of receiving a pre-digested Masonry ladled out to him by another should make his own Masonry for himself by study and reflection upon the work and the symbols. Thus he stood for thorough going individual Masonic development. He stood for a Masonry built up within each Mason by himself and for himself on the solid foundation of internal conviction. This Masonic Protestantism, as it might well be called, is especially interesting in one who was so thoroughly filled with French writings upon Masonry. Secondly he gave us a genuine interpretation of the symbols which came into Masonry through the hermetic philosophers. Hutchinson and Preston and even Oliver in many cases did not understand these symbols at all. Indeed Preston was much less interested in what they really were than in how they might be made instruments of education in his time and place. Accordingly Preston and Oliver gave currency to inadequate and often ignorant explanations of ancient symbols. Pike studied their history and development. He mastered their spirit and perceived their place in the evolution of human thinking. Hence he was able to replace the crude symbolism of the end of the eighteenth century by a real science of Masonic symbols. In the third place not only did he interpret our symbols but he enriched the symbolism of the Craft from a profound acquaintance with the ancient and modern literature of symbolism and mysticism. Thus he made us aware that the science of Masonic symbols is but part of a much wider subject, that it is not self-sufficient and that the serious Masonic Student has much more to study than he can find within the covers of an exclusively Masonic library.

    I can do no more than give you a key to what I conceive to be Pike's philosophy of Masonry. Perhaps the first point to make is that in nineteenth-century America philosophy was regarded, under the influence of Herbert Spencer, as the unification of knowledge. Moreover the metaphysical method of the first half of the nineteenth century, when Pike's ideas were formative, was to endeavor to explain everything in a "speculative, metaphysical way by a spiritual, logical principle." But it so happened that all antiquity had been making a like search for the One but for a different sort of One. The earlier Greek philosophers sought a single element to which the whole universe might be reduced. The Ionian philosophers sought to find such elements in air or fire or water or, as one of them put it, "a primordial slime." Oriental thinkers had usually sought an absolute word which was to be the key of all things. Others among the ancients had sought an absolute principle. With vast labor Pike brings together all that ancient and Oriental peoples thought and wrote and all that mystics have since thought and written with the ideas of the Orient and of antiquity as a basis and upon this foundation he sets forth to work out a system of his own.

Pike starts with a triad. This is suggested by the ancient conception of the number three as the symbol of completion or perfection. The singular, the dual and the plural, the odd and even added, was thought of as a complete system of numbers. Hence the number three was perfection in its simplest form; it was the type or the symbol of perfection. He finds a triad everywhere in ancient thought and in every system of the occult and in every mystic philosophy. He finds it also in all Masonic symbolism and from end to end in our lectures. Accordingly he seeks to show that in its essentials this triad is at all times and in all its forms the same triad. Wisdom, strength, beauty; intelligence, force, harmony; reason, will, action; morals, law, social order; faith, hope, charity; equality, liberty, fraternity--all these he shows are the same triad in various forms. There is a fruitful passive principle which is energized and made productive by an active, creative principle and there is a product. As he shows, Osiris, Isis and Horus symbolize this with the Egyptians and he traces the same reduction of the universe to these fundamental through every type of ancient mystery and all mystic speculation. In Morals and Dogma he makes all manner of application of this idea to politics, to morals and to religion. He carries it into every type of human spiritual activity and gives the most copious and learned illustrations.

But this of itself would be barren and would end in pluralism. Accordingly he conceives that these three things are emanations, or better, are manifestations of the Absolute. This idea again he subjects to the test of application to all that has been thought and written by mystics down to his time. We find a unity in the Absolute. But how do we unify the manifold, the infinite manifestations of the Absolute in our experience ? Is there here some one principle? Pike says there is and that this unifying principle is equilibrium or balance. The result of the action of creative, active energy and productive, passive receptivity is in the end a harmony, a balance, an equilibrium. He then applies this idea of equilibrium to every field of thought. One example will suffice.

"It is the Secret of the Universal Equilibrium:--

"Of that Equilibrium in the Deity, between the Infinite Divine Wisdom and the Infinite Divine Power, from which result the Stability of the Universe, the unchangeableness of the Divine Law, and the Principles of Truth, Justice, and Right which are a part of it;
. . .

"Of that Equilibrium also, between the Infinite Divine Justice and the Infinite Divine Mercy, the result of which is the Infinite Divine Equity, and the M oral Harmony or Beauty of the Universe. By it the endurance of created and imperfect natures in the presence of a Perfect Deity is made possible;

"Of that Equilibrium between Necessity and Liberty, between the action of the Divine Omnipotence and the Free-will of man, by which vices and base actions, and ungenerous thoughts and words are crimes and wrongs, justly punished by the law of cause and consequence, though nothing in the Universe can happen or be done contrary to the will of God; and without which co-existence of Liberty and Necessity, of Freewill in the creature and Omnipotence in the Creator, there could be no religion, nor any law of right and wrong, or merit and demerit, nor any justice in human punishments or penal laws.

"Of that Equilibrium between Good and Evil, and Light and Darkness in the world, which assures us that all is the work of the Infinite Wisdom and of an Infinite Love; and that there is no rebellious demon of Evil, or Principle of Darkness co-existent and in eternal controversy with God, or the Principle of Light and of Good: by attaining to the knowledge of which equilibrium we can, through Faith, see that the existence of Evil, sin, Suffering, and Sorrow in the world, is consistent with the Infinite Goodness as well as with the Infinite Wisdom of the Almighty.

"Sympathy and Antipathy, Attraction and Repulsion, each a Force of nature, are contraries, in the souls of men and in the universe of spheres and worlds; and from the action and opposition of each against the other, result Harmony, and that movement which is the Life of the Universe and the Soul alike...

"Of that Equilibrium between Authority and Individual Action which constitutes Free Government, by settling on immutable foundations Liberty with Obedience to Law, Equality with Subjection to Authority, and Fraternity with Subordination to the wisest and the Best: and of that Equilibrium between the Active Energy of the Will of the Present, expressed by the Vote of the People, and the Passive Stability and Permanence of the Will of the Past, expressed in constitutions of government, written or unwritten, and in the laws and customs, gray with age and sanctified by time, as precedents and authority;

"And, finally, of that Equilibrium, possible in ourselves, and which Masonry incessantly labors to accomplish in its Initiates, and demands of its Adepts and Princes (else unworthy of their titles), between the Spiritual and Divine and the Material and Human in man; between the Intellect, Reason, and Moral Sense on one side, and the Appetites and Passions on the other, from which result the Harmony and Beauty of a well-regulated life."

Well, we have got our idea of equilibrium and the profane will say: What of it ? Pike would answer that this universal unifying principle is the light of which all men in all ages have been in search, the light which we seek as Masons. Hence we get our answers to the fundamental problems of Masonic philosophy.

1) What is the end of Masonry? What is the purpose for which it exists? Pike would answer: the immediate end is the pursuit of light. But light means here attainment of the fundamental principle of the universe and bringing of ourselves into the harmony, the ultimate unity which alone is real. Hence the ultimate end is to lead us to the Absolute--interpreted by our individual creed if we like but recognized as the final unity into which all things merge and with which in the end all things must accord. You will see here at once a purely philosophical version of what, with Oliver, was purely religious.

2) What is the relation of Masonry to other human institutions and particularly to the state and to religion? He would answer it seeks to interpret them to us, to make them more vital for us, to make them more efficacious for their purposes by showing

the ultimate reality of which they are manifestations. It teaches us that there is but one Absolute and that everything short of that Absolute is relative; is but a manifestation, so that creeds and dogmas, political or religious, are but interpretations. It teaches us to make our own interpretation for ourselves. It teaches us to save ourselves by finding for ourselves the ultimate principle by which we shall come to the real. In other words, it is the universal institution of which other spiritual, moral and social institutions are local and temporary phases.

3) How does Masonry seek to reach these ends? He would say by a system of allegories and of symbols handed down from antiquity which we are to study and upon which we are to reflect until they reveal the light to each of us individually. Masonry preserves these symbols and acts out these allegories for us. But the responsibility of reaching the real through them is upon each of us. Each of us has the duty of using this wonderful heritage from antiquity for himself. Masonry in Pike's view does not offer us predigested food. It offers us a wholesome fare which we must digest for ourselves. But what a feast ! It is nothing less than the whole history of human search for reality. And through it he conceives, through mastery of it, we shall master the universe.

PART V
A TWENTIETH-CENTURY MASONIC PHILOSOPHY

We have long outgrown the notion that Masonry is to be held to one purpose or one object or is to be hemmed in by the confines of one philosophy. If we are taught truly that the roof of the Mason's workshop is nothing less than the "clouded canopy or starry-decked heavens," nothing that goes on beneath that capacious covering can be wholly alien to us. Our Fraternity is to be of all men and for all men; it is to be of all time and for all time. The needs of no one time and of no one people can circumscribe its objects. The philosophy of no one time, of no one people, and much more of no one man, can be admitted as its final authority. Hence it is no reproach to Masonry to have, along with lessons and tenets for all times, a special lesson and a special tenet for each time, which is not to be insisted on at other times. Truth, after all, is relative. Vital truths to one time cannot be put into pellets or boluses to be administered to all times to come. If the Craft is to be perpetual, it must appeal to each time as well as to all times; it must have in its traditions something that today can use, although yesterday could not use it and tomorrow need not. We are a Craft of workmen. It is our glory to be engaged in useful service. Our rites and usages are not merely a proud possession to be treasured for their beauty and antiquity. They are instruments imparted to us to be used. Hence we may properly inquire, what can we make of this wonderful tradition of which we are the custodians that will serve the world of today?

One is indeed rash who essays a philosophy of Masonry after such masters as Krause and Oliver and Pike. But I have tried to show heretofore how largely their philosophies of Masonry grew out of the time and the philosophical situation at the time when they severally thought and wrote. Thus Preston wrote in the so-called "age of reason," when Knowledge was supposed to be the one thing needful. Krause wrote moral philosophy, so-called, was a chief concern in Germany, and he was primarily a leader in the philosophy of law. Oliver wrote under the influence of Romanticism in England, at a time when German idealism was coming into English thought. Pike wrote under the influence of the reaction from the materialism of last half of the nineteenth century and under the influence of the nineteenth century metaphysical method of unifying all things by reference to some basic absolute principle.

In the same way a present-day philosophy of Masonry will necessarily relate itself to present-day modes of thought and to the present situation in philosophy. Consequently we may predict that it will have four characteristics.

1) Its metaphysical creed will be either idealistic-monistic--or else pragmatist-pluralistic. Although my personal sympathies are with the latter view, so that in a sense I should range myself with Preston and Krause rather than with Oliver and Pike,

I suspect that our twentieth-century Masonic philosopher will adhere to the former. He will probably hold, to quote Paulsen, that "reality, which is represented to our senses by the corporeal world as a uniform system of movements, is the manifestation of a universal spiritual life that is to be conceived as an idea, as the development of a unitary reason, a reason which infinitely transcends our notions." Hence he will probably range himself with Oliver and Pike. But he will despair of comprehending this reason through knowledge or through tradition or of completely expressing it in a single word. And so, if by chance he should be a pragmatist, the result will not be very different, since the philosophy of Masonry is a part of applied philosophy and the results count for more than the exact method of attaining them. Moreover in the three following characteristics, idealist and pragmatist will agree, merely coming to the same results by different routes.

2) Its psychology will be voluntaristic rather than intellectualistic; that is, under the influence of modern biology it will insist upon giving a chief place to the will. It will have faith in the efficacy of conscious human effort.

3) What is more important for our purpose, its standpoint will be teleological. To quote Paulsen once more: "Ethics and sociology, jurisprudence and politics are about to give up the old formalistic treatment and to employ instead the teleological method: purpose governs life, hence the science of life, of individual as well as of collective life, must employ

this principle." In other words, as it would have been put formerly, the philosophy of Masonry will be treated as a part of practical rather than of pure philosophy.

4) It will have its roots in history. This is the distinguishing mark of modern philosophical thought. The older philosophies conceived of reality along the lines of mathematics and of the physical sciences. Today we endeavor to interpret nature historically. As Paulsen says, we essay to interpret it "according to a logical genetical scheme."

Such are the lines which modern philosophy is following, and such, we may be confident, are the lines which the philosophy of Masonry will follow, unless, indeed, some philosopher of the stamp of Krause, capable of striking out new paths in philosophy at large, should busy himself with this special field. Can we construct a philosophy of Masonry that will conform to these lines ? In attempting to answer this question, I should lay down three fundamental principles at the outset:

1) We must not be dogmatic. We must remember that our ideal is the ideal of an epoch, to serve the needs of time and place.

2) Nevertheless we must seek an end. We must have before us the idea of purpose, since we are in the realm of practical philosophy.

3) We must base our conception of the ideal of our Masonic epoch and our idea of purpose upon the history of institutions. Thus we get three modes of approach to our immediate subject.

Let us first turn to the current philosophies and inquire what they may do for us. How far may we build on some one or on all of them? What does Masonry call for which they can or cannot give?

1) The oldest and perhaps the most authoritative system of philosophy current today is absolute idealism, in many forms, indeed, but with a recognizable essential unity. This philosophy puts life in a world of thought. It thinks of the world of experience which we perceive through our senses as appearance. Reality is in the world of thought. But these are not two distinct worlds. Rather they are related as cause and effect, as that which animates and that which is animated. It regards God, not as a power outside of the world and transcending it, but as that which permeates it and connects it and gives it unity. It regards reality as a connected, a unified whole and conceives that life is real in so far as it is a part of this whole. Hence it conceives we must turn steadfastly and courageously from the superficial realm of appearance in which our senses put us, and set ourselves "in the depth of reality"; we are to bring ourselves into relation with the whole and to develop ourselves from within so as to reach the whole. To use Eucken's phrases, each life is to "evolve a morality in the sense of taking up the whole into one's own volition" and subjecting "caprice to the necessity of things," that is, to their necessary inner interconnection. In this theory of life, the central point is spiritual creative activity. Everything else is but the environment, the means or the logical

presupposition. Man is to be raised above himself and is to be saved by spiritual creation.

This philosophy of scholars and for scholars is not a philosophy for Masons. Indeed Pike said of his idealistic system of Masonic philosophy that it was not the Masonry of the multitude. And for this very reason that it is essentially aristocratic, the old idealistic philosophy is fighting a sure though obstinate retreat in our democratic age. There are periods of creative energy in the world and there are periods in which what has been created is organized and assimilated. In the periods of creation, those to whom spiritual creative power is given are relatively few. In a period of assimilation they are few indeed. In such a time, to quote Eucken, the life pictured by the idealist "tends to become mere imagination." "The man imbued with [its] spirit . . . easily seems to himself more than he is; with a false self-consciousness talks and feels as if he were at a supreme height; lives less his own life than an alien one. Sooner or later opposition must necessarily arise against such a half life, such a life of pretense, and this opposition will become especially strong if it is animated by the desire that all who bear human features should participate in the chief goods of our existence and freely co-operate in the highest tasks. . . And so the aristocratic character of Immanent Idealism produces a type of life rigidly exclusive, harsh and intolerable."

Another type of philosophy, which has become more and more current with the advance of science, has been called Naturalism. This philosophy rejects the spiritual life entirely, denying its independence and holding it nothing but a phase or an incident of the existence revealed by the senses. There is no spiritual sphere. Of itself, the spiritual can create nothing. Nor is life anything in itself. All things are valued in terms of biology and of economics. Nothing is intrinsically valuable. Truth means only correct adjustment to the environment; the good is that which best preserves life; the moral is that which makes for social life; the beautiful is a form of the useful. Self preservation is the real inspiration of conduct. I need not argue that this is not a philosophy for Masons, who have faith in God for one of their landmarks. Whatever else we may be consistently with a naturalistic philosophy, we cannot be Masons. For if there is any one test of a Mason it is a test wholly incompatible with this rejection of the spiritual.

Closely connected with naturalism are a variety of social philosophies which have come to have much vogue and in one form, socialism, have given rise to an active propaganda involving almost religious fervor. These philosophies reject the individual life, and hence the individual spiritual life. So far as the individual will is regarded it is because of a social interest in the individual social life. As political or social philosophies some of these systems have very great value. But when they are expanded into universal systems and make material welfare in society--a very proper end in political philosophy--

the sole end of the individual life, when they reject the spiritual independence of the individual by making "the judgment of society the test of truth" and expect him to submit his views of good and evil to the arbitrament of a show of hands, when they ignore individual creation and think only of distributing, they run counter to Masonic landmarks, so that we cannot accept them and continue to be Masons. For we hold as Masons that there is a spiritual part of man. We hold that the individual is to construct a moral and spiritual edifice within himself by earnest labor, not to receive one ready-made by a referendum to the judgment of society. Understand me. I do not assert that modern social philosophies are to be cast out utterly. In law, in politics, in social science some of them are achieving great things. But we must think of them as applications, not as universal systems. The problem of the individual life, the demands of the individual spiritual life, which they ignore, are matters of vital concern to the Mason, and he calls for a philosophy which takes account of them. To quote Eucken once more, we cannot assent that the "world of sense is the sole world of man" nor can we "find life entirely in the relation to the environment, be it nature or society."

By way of revolt from naturalistic and social philosophies a modern movement has arisen which has been called aesthetic individualism. It is distinctly a literary and artistic movement and for that very reason ignores the mass of humanity and falls short of our basic Masonic requirement of universality. But it demands a moment's consideration as one of the significant modes of modern thought. In aesthetic individualism, we are told, "the center of life is transferred into the inner tissue of self-consciousness. With the development of this self-consciousness, life appears to be placed entirely on its own resources and directed towards itself. Through all change of circumstances and conditions it remains undisturbed; in all the infinity of that which happens to it, it feels that it is supreme. All external manifestation is valuable to it as an unfolding of its own being; it never experiences things, but only itself." Hence to the aesthetic individualist the end is to "make all the relations and all the externals of life as individual as possible." He is not to sacrifice the present to the future; he is to reject everything that subjects the development of life to universal standards; he is to ignore all those conventions that fit men into the social order and instead is to cultivate a free relation of individual to individual. To those who accept this doctrine "what is usually called morality is considered to be only a statute of the community, a means by which it seeks to rob the individualist the end is to "make all the relations and all the itself." This philosophy of artists and for artists is too palpably impossible for the Masonic philosopher to require further discussion.

If we turn from these disappointing modern theories of the end of life to systems of applied philosophy, we may do better. Here the idealists have a more fruitful program. Where Hegel regarded all things as the unfolding of an idea either logically or in experience, the recent followers of Hegel, who are the most active force in recent social philosophy, say rather that all social and political and legal institutions are manifestations of civilization. To them the idea which is unfolding in all things human is not some single metaphysical principle; it is the complex idea of human civilization. Our institutions are resultants of the civilization of the past and of attempts to adapt them as we received them, to the civilization of the present. Our task as members of society is to advance civilization by exerting ourselves consciously and intelligently to that end. Every man may do this in some measure in his time and place. So every man may, if he will, retard or obstruct civilization in some degree in his time and place. But from the fact that he is a man and as such a factor in society actually or potentially, he is charged with a duty of exerting himself to maintain and advance civilization, of which as the ultimate idea, society is a mere agent. So far as we may, we must each of us discover the principles which are presupposed by the civilization of today and we must exert ourselves consciously to mold institutions thereto and to regulate conduct thereby. The universal thing, the reality is civilization among men. To paraphrase a well-known formula, God is the eternal, not ourselves, that makes for civilization. Here, then, we have a modern system that comports with the fundamenta of Masonry and with our philosophical demands. It recognizes the spiritual side of man as something which civilization both presupposes and develops. It has a God. It is not for a scholarly or artistic aristocracy. It is of and for all men as partakers in and, if they will be, agents of a universal human culture. Moreover it meets our first requirement. It is not dogmatic. It recognizes that civilization is something that is constantly advancing and hence is changing. It realizes that civilization, for that very reason, is a matter of time and place and hence that the principles it presupposes at any time and place, which we take for our ideals, are ideals of an epoch and principles to serve the needs of time and place. And yet all these stages transient forms of human culture merge in a general and a constantly growing human civilization which is the reality both in ourselves and outside of ourselves.

2) Again the new idealism of practical philosophy meets our second requirement. Even though its adherents recognize that they have no absolute formula for all times, for all places, for all peoples, they have an end, they put before us a purpose. Each of us and all of us are to make for human civilization. Each of us by developing himself as a civilized, in the real sense, as a cultured man according to his lights and his circumstances can find reality in himself and can bring others and the whole nearer to the reality for which we are consciously or unconsciously striving--the civilization of mankind. The knowledge which Preston sought to advance, the perfection of man at which Krause aimed, the relation to God which Oliver sought to attain and the harmony and

through it control of the universe which Pike took for the goal, may well be regarded as phases of and as summed up in the one idea of human civilization.

3) How far does this new idealism, or as its adherents call it, this neo-Hegelianism, meet our third requirement? Has it a sound basis in the history of human institutions generally and the history of our institution in particular? Here at least the Masonic neo-idealist is upon sure ground.

Anthropologists and sociologists have shown us that next to the family, which indeed antedates society, the most primitive and most universal of social institutions is the association of grown men in a secret society. The simplest and earliest of the institutions of social man is the "men's house"--a separate house for the men of the tribe which has some analogies among civilized peoples of antiquity, e.g. the common meal of the citizens at Sparta, the assembly of the men in the agora in an ancient Greek community and the meeting of the Roman citizens in assembly in the ancient polity of the Roman city. In this men's house of a primitive tribe is the center of social life. Here the most precious belongings of the community, its religious emblems and its trophies taken in war, are preserved. Here the young men of the tribe gather as a visible token of their separation from their families and their entrance upon the duties and responsibilities of tribal life. Here the elders and leaders have seats according to their dignity and importance. Women and children may not enter; it is the house of the grown men. This wide-spread primitive institution develops in different ways. Sometimes it results in what are practically barracks for the fighting men of the community, as at Sparta and among some primitive peoples today. Sometimes it becomes a religious center and ultimately in substance a temple. Usually it becomes the center of another stage of social development, that is, of what anthropologists call "the puberty initiation ceremonies" and thence of still another stage, the primitive secret society. And as these societies develop, replacing the earlier tribal puberty initiations, the men's house, as the seat of these organizations, becomes the secret lodge. Hence in this oldest of social institutions, rather than on the highest hills and in the lowest dales of our lectures, we may find the first Masonry.

It is a natural instinct, so sociologists tell us, that leads men of the same age, who have the same interests and the same duties, to group themselves accordingly and to separate to some extent from other groups. In obedience to this instinct, we are told that four classes of the male members of a tribe set themselves off:

1) The boys who have not yet arrived at puberty

2) unmarried youths

3) mature men on whom the duties and responsibilities of tribesmen rest, and

4) old men, the repositories of tribal wisdom and the directors of the community.

On the attainment of puberty, the boy is taken

into the men's house and as it were initiated into manhood. In due time he becomes tribesman and warrior. In process of time his eldest son has himself reached manhood and the father becomes an elder, retired from active service. Thus the men of the tribe become in substance a secret association divided into two or three grades or classes out of which, we are told, as a later development, grow the degrees of primitive secret societies. For the passage from one of these classes to another almost universally among primitive peoples is accompanied by secret initiatory ceremonies, and among almost all primitive peoples, the initiatory ceremonies at puberty are the most solemn and important event in a man's life. Usually they are more or less dramatic. They begin with some sort of ordeal. Often there is a symbolic raising from death to life to show that the child is dead and that a man has risen in his place. Often a great deal of symbolism is employed and there follows something very like a lecture, explaining the ceremony. Always they involve an impressive instruction in the science and the morality of the tribe and an impressive inculcation of obedience.

In time these initiatory ceremonies degenerate or develop, as the case may be, into tribal secret societies pure and simple, and with the progress of civilization and the rise of political and religious systems these societies also decay or lose their character. Thus eventually, out of this primitive institution of the men's house, which on one side has grown into political organization, on another side, through the initiatory ceremonies, no less than six institutions are developed among different peoples. First there are political, magical and more or less fraudulent secret societies, which are extremely common in Africa today. Second, there are clan ceremonies, becoming in time state ceremonies and state religions. Antiquity abounds in examples of the importance which men attached to these ceremonies. For example, the dictator Fabius, at a critical moment in the campaign against Hannibal, left the army in order to repair to the proper place and perform the clan sacrifices as head of the Fabian gens. Third, there are religious societies, with elaborate ceremonies for the reception of the novice. Such societies exist in Tibet and among the Hindus in striking forms. Fourth, there are the mysteries of antiquity, for example, the Egyptian and the Eleusinian, or sometimes a mixture of the third and fourth, as in the case of the Essenes. Fifth, there are trade societies on the fraternal model, such as the Roman collegia and the trade and operative guilds. Finally there are purely charitable associations, such as the Roman burial societies. Each of these, it will be noted, develops or preserves some side of the primitive tribal secret society. The political and magical societies develop or preserve their political and medical traditions; the clan ceremonies, their function of promoting solidarity by ancestor worship; the religious societies, their moral and religious functions; the mysteries, their symbolical instruction; the trade societies, their function of instruction in useful knowledge; the charitable societies, their function of binding men to duties of relief and of mutual assistance. All preserve the memory of their origin in a tribe of kinsmen by the fiction of brotherhood which they strive to make real by teaching and practice.

The relation of Masonry to this development of societies out of the primitive men's house, as described by non-Masonic scholars with no thought of Masonry, is so obvious, that we may no longer laugh at Oliver's ambitious attempts to find Masonry in the very beginning of things. But apart from its bearing upon Masonic history, this discovery of the anthropologists is significant for Masonic philosophy. For in this same men's house are the germs of civilization; the development of the men's house is a development of civilization, and its end and purpose and the end and purpose of all the legitimate institutions that have grown out of it have been from the beginning to preserve, further and hand down the civilization of the tribe or people. In our universal society, therefore, the end is, and as we study our old charges and our lectures we see it has always been, to preserve, further and hand down a universal, human civilization.

Thus we are enabled to answer the three problems of Masonic philosophy.

1) What is the end of Masonry; for what do we exist as an organization? The answer of the Masonic neo-idealist would be that our end in common with all social institutions is to preserve, to develop and to transmit to posterity the civilization wrought by our

fathers and passed on to us.

2) What is the place of Masonry in a rational scheme of human activity ? What is its relation to other kindred activities? The answer would be, that it is an organization of human effort along the universal lines on which all may agree in order to realize our faith in the efficacy of conscious effort in preserving and promoting civilization. What other human organizations do along lines of caste or creed or within political or territorial limits hampered by the limits of political feeling or local prejudice, we seek to achieve by universality--by organizing the universal elements in man that make for culture and civilization.

3) How does Masonry achieve its end? Our answer would be that it makes for civilization by its insistence on the solidarity of humanity, by its insistence on universality and by the preservation and transmission of an immemorial tradition of human solidarity and of universality. So conceived, this tradition becomes a force of the first moment in maintaining and advancing civilization. And in this way we connect on the one hand with the practical systems of Preston and of Krause. The ideal of the eighteenth century was knowledge. The ideal of the nineteenth century was the individual moral life. The ideal of the twentieth century, I take it, is the universal human life. But what are these but means toward the advance of human culture? And on the other hand we connect also with Oliver and with Pike. For they were idealists and so are we. Only they

sought a simple, static idea of which the universe was a manifestation or an unfolding. We turn rather to a complex and growing idea and claim to do no more than interpret it in terms of the ideals of the time and place.

My brethren, we of all men, owe it to ourselves and to the world, to be universal in spirit. Universality is a lesson the whole world is learning and must learn. But we ought to know it well already. We ought to be upon the front bench of the world's school, setting an example to our more backward school-fellows. Wherever in the world there is a lodge of Masons, there should be a focus of civilization, a center of the idea of universality, radiating reason to put down prejudice and advance justice in the disputes of peoples, and in the disputes of classes, and making for the peace and harmony and civilization that should prevail in this great lodge of the world.

Moreover, the idea of universality has a special message to the Mason for the good of Masonry. Every world-organization hitherto has been wrecked ultimately upon its own dogmatism. It has taken the dogmas, the interpretations, the philosophy of its youth for a fixed order of nature. It has assumed that universality consisted in forcing these dogmas, these interpretations, this philosophy upon all times to come. While it has rested serene in the ruts made by its own prosperity, the world has marched by it unseen. We have a glorious body of tradition handed down to us from the past, which we owe it to transmit unimpaired to the future. But let us understand what in it is fundamental and eternal, and what is mere interpretation to make it of service to the past. Let us while we have it use it well to make it of service to the present. Yet let us fasten upon it nothing hard and fast that serves well enough to make it useful today, but may make it useless tomorrow. As the apprentice stands in the corner of the lodge, the working tools are put in his hands and he is taught their uses. But they are not his. They are the tools of the lodge. He is to use them that the Worshipful Master may have pleasure and the Craft profit. The Grand Master of the Universe has entrusted to us the principles of Masonry as working tools. They, too, are not ours, they belong to the lodge of the world. We are to use them that He may have pleasure and the Craft of humanity that labors in this wide lodge of the world may profit thereby.

www.ingramcontent.com/pod-product-compliance
Lightning Source LLC
Chambersburg PA
CBHW021018090426
42738CB00007B/821